For Love of the Motorcycle

For Love of the Motorcycle

T. J. Overstake

ISBN 978-0-557-85049-5

Contents

For Love of the Motorcycle 1

The Super Hawk 5

The 650 Special.. 15

The TLR200s 21

Police Motorcycle Stories 33

The Fiesta Bowl Parade 37

The Flower Boy 47

The Sick Lawyer 57

The RTX'es.. 67

Sight Unseen Motorcycles 77

Victory 81

Capo 85

Nearly Famous on a Police Bike...................................... 89

Sir Charles... 95

Devon... 101

Vern... 105

Conclusion 113

For Love of the Motorcycle

I took off my rings a few minutes ago. I wear one on the ring finger of each hand, my wedding ring and my Police service ring. I knew I'd be typing, and I didn't want to cause sparks.

I never learned how to type in the correct manner. People who can type without actually looking at the keyboard always struck me as impossible. I know what I can and cannot do. Wasting time on things I don't think I can do, or a thing I don't think I can master, always seemed a waste of time. I figure I have a finite number of brain cells. Once they're full it's either stop learning things or make room for new stuff by forgetting old stuff. Anyway, that's a long-winded way to say I never learned to type the right way. I have to look at the keys while I type and, since I type very quickly, my fingers bang into each other as I type. So I take off my rings.

I waited until I was nearly fifty years old to write my first book. I always wanted to write a book, and I've a million stories floating around in my head. I was asked a hundred times why I never wrote a book. I finally decided to write one, and last year I finished it. It was a fun book filled with cool stories about all the cars I owned over the last 35 years.

My first book was called 'For Love of the Car', and it was very well received. I actually sold some copies and everyone I met who read it really liked it. I started off by giving copies to friends and family members. They all loved the book and told me so. I was even asked to sign a bunch of them.

While I've always been known as a 'Car Guy', I've owned a great number of motorcycles too. Though not as numerous as my cars, I've still had a ton of bikes. All sorts of bikes; big bikes, small bikes, road bikes, dirt bikes and everything in-between. I always loved motorcycles and even have three of them in the garage right now. I replaced the carburetor on one last night and have some parts on order to help make another one road-worthy.

There's nothing like riding a motorcycle. It's a shame, there are so many people who'll never experience the thrill of two-wheeling.

The freedom, the open-airiness, the sights and sounds and, well, you get the idea. Don't get me wrong. I know motorcycling isn't for everyone.

For one thing, it's dangerous.

There's always someone out there, consciously or not, trying to kill you. There are so many people not paying attention; reading, texting, applying makeup, talking on the phone, cursing unruly kids or simply daydreaming. There are a million ways for someone in a car to become distracted enough to kill a motorcyclist.

For another thing, it's uncomfortable.

I've taken thousands of motorcycle rides in my life. Some are vivid in my mind to this very day. I remember riding in the worst Arizona dust storms, the strongest horizontal rain, the most bitterly cold nights and the blistering desert heat. There's always something. I don't recall there being many perfect rides. Not really. Something always happens on a motorcycle ride that could never happen in a car.

I can't remember the last time my butt hurt after an hour behind the wheel in a car. I can't remember a car making my wrists hurt, my back ache or my eyes water. Car driving never gets too cold or too hot. Car driving never scares the shit out of you when you cross railroad tracks or hit a pothole. You never get the feeling the wind is actually blowing hard enough to topple you when you're in a car. Stuff doesn't get stuck in your teeth while driving a car. Bugs, rocks and cigarette butts never hit you in the chops when you drive a car. All of those things happen on a motorcycle.

Easy to see why I love motorcycles so much, huh? Yeah, I know but, until the bike bug bites you, you just have to trust guys like me who have already been bitten.

All in all, I think I'm as much a Bike Guy as I am a Car Guy. My first vehicle was a motorcycle. The worst injuries I've ever had were from riding motorcycles. I rode a motorcycle professionally for almost 15 years. I bought them new, I bought them old and I bought them in boxes full of pieces. I've owned bikes I was never able to ride, and I've owned bikes I could never get enough of riding. I've ridden bikes because I had to, and I've ridden simply because I wanted to. I've ridden bikes to get places, and I've ridden bikes to go absolutely nowhere in particular.

Yeah, I'm a Bike Guy.

Knowing this about me, most of my friends and family asked me why I didn't write a book about the bikes, too. Well, I've succumbed.

This is a book about my motorcycles. Welcome to 'For Love of the Motorcycle'. There are such cool stories about so many of my bikes I could tell them for you all day.

How's that for an introduction?

Let's get started.

The Super Hawk

In the summer of 1974 I was 15 and a half years old and wanted a car so bad I could taste it. Lots of my friends were 16 already and were driving cars. I envied them so much it kept me up at night. I thought of nothing but cars all day long. I think a lot of kids my age did, especially in the beautiful northern California area where we lived at the time. We lived just outside San Jose, in a town called Campbell, California. This was a wonderful town that had wide, well maintained roads and fine scenery with plenty of places to go and countless things to do. It seemed the whole town was always on the move.

Dad had a nice Ford Torino he was teaching me to drive in. I had a learner's permit and Dad actually let me drive from time to time. I loved driving, and Dad was great about letting me drive, but I still wanted my own car. I wanted a car so, so bad but at least until I was sixteen I'd have to wait.

For a car that is.

In California, there was a licensing rule allowing a new driver with a learner's permit to ride a motorcycle, all alone, during daylight hours. I guess they figured it was too tough to learn to ride a motorcycle with a coach grabbing you from behind by the ribs. Whatever the reason, the rule was there and some of my not-quite-sixteen year old friends were doing it. My friend Russell was one of these newbie bikers.

Russell had a cool old BMW motorcycle he rode to school each day. He even rode it to the golf course on the weekends, with his golf bag slung over his shoulder. It had faded black paint, was missing some pieces and for some reason Russ stuck old tube socks into the open throats of the carburetors when he parked it. Without air cleaners installed, I think he was afraid bugs would get in there. Anyway, Russell loved his bike and convinced me I should have one too. Bikes, Russell explained, were cheap to buy, economical to own and inexpensive to insure. Best of all, at fifteen and a half years old, I could ride one right away.

It didn't take any more convincing than that. I wanted a car, but a motorcycle would do until I was old enough for a car. I had some money because I lied about my age and got a summer job at a local drug store stocking shelves. Yep, a motorcycle was a good idea.

Why not?

The first thing I had to do was convince Mom and Dad I should have a motorcycle. As it turned out, I don't remember Mom and Dad had too many objections to it. Yeah, I know. I remember being surprised, too. I had to promise to be careful, to buy my own insurance and, most importantly, pay for it myself. Aside from that, convincing them to let me ride a motorcycle wasn't too hard at all. Maybe they thought I was joking, or maybe they thought I'd get discouraged when I couldn't find a bike I could afford. Whatever the reason, I had their okay. My hunt for a motorcycle started right away.

I didn't wait long. Ben, one of the guys at the store, had an old bike at home he didn't ride anymore. He dropped it and damaged it one day and simply stopped riding it. It was parked alongside the house and hadn't been ridden in months. If I wanted to come by and take a look at it, he'd make me a good deal on it.

As soon as I could I rode my bicycle to his house to see the motorcycle. As promised, it was under a canvas tarp leaning up against the side of the house. The return spring on the kickstand was broken and Ben found it easier to simply lean it up against the house than to fix the kickstand.

When he pulled the tarp off, I remember thinking this was one funky looking bike. I'd never seen anything quite like it. I knew guys that rode motocross bikes, like Bultacos and Pentons, but this was no motocross bike. I knew other guys who rode sport bikes, like Triumphs and BSAs. This was no sport bike.

No, this was a 1966 Honda Super Hawk, and it was weird looking. It had big rounded fenders that made the bike look like it was wearing some kind of metallic spats over its tires. It also had a big, fat, puffy seat that looked like it was designed for a very, very big butt. The headlight housing, called a nacelle, was huge and stuck out ahead of the handlebars in cartoon-like fashion. The bike was painted jet black and had shiny chrome wheels, chrome side panels on its odd shaped gas tank and high, chrome handlebars. There was a big plastic knob atop those handlebars that would make loud clicks as you rotated it back and forth. The knob had something to do with steering dampening but Ben said as long as he'd owned the bike he couldn't figure out what, if anything, the knob actually did.

Aside from being funky looking, the bike also wouldn't start. The kick-starter was broken. When Ben last dropped the bike it fell over on its side. The engine case hit the ground hard enough to crack it and the gears in the kick-starter wouldn't mesh anymore. When he tried to use the kick-starter all it did was make a nasty grinding sound before ended up pointing straight at the ground like a second kickstand. The only way to start the bike was to use the electric starter or, since the bike's battery was dead, to push-start it.

Okay.

"No, it's not that hard. I'll show you. Let's push it out into the street".

We pushed the bike down the driveway and into the street in front of the house. It was a quiet residential street and was perfect for pushing an old, heavy, damaged motorcycle. Ben turned the key, opened the fuel valve, twisted the throttle a couple of times, closed the choke and said, "Get on."

I hesitated, just a bit.

"You ever push-started a bike before?" Ben asked.

"No. I've never even ridden one before"

"What? I thought you knew how to ride".

"Nope, never even sat on one before".

Well, this certainly made a difference. I'm really not sure what I expected. I knew I wanted to see Ben's bike, and I knew I wanted to buy one, but I don't think I gave much thought to actually riding one. I'd never ridden a real, street-legal motorcycle before. Some of my friends had little motorbikes we rode in dirt lots. These had little lawn-mower type engines in them. We started them by pulling on a rope. These mini-bikes were tiny things too, not much more than two feet tall. They were slow and I don't think they even had brakes. We called them Tote Goats, after the company that made nice ones that were sold in stores, even though the ones we rode were largely home made. This was as close as I ever came to riding a motorcycle. I don't even think I was very good at Tote Goat riding. I have no idea what made me think I could ride a motorcycle.

"You can ride a bicycle, can't you?" Ben asked.

"Sure", I said. I was the best bicycle rider I knew. I even had a part-time job at my neighborhood bicycle shop, the Pedal and Wheel on Campbell Avenue. I knew about bicycles. I rode one every day, everywhere I went.

"It's not much different than riding a bicycle", Ben assured me.

I thus began my first and only motorcycle lesson. Ben wanted to sell me that motorcycle, and he wasn't going to let a simple thing like me not knowing how to ride stop him. Without hesitation Ben began to describe to operation of the motorcycle's controls. I was shown the two tiny pedals that operated the rear brake and the gear shifter. I learned about the 3-position ignition switch, the light switch and the handlebar switches. I even learned, if the battery was good, there was a tiny black button that would engage the starter and if all was right, bring the little 305cc twin cylinder motor to life. I also learned about the clutch and front brakes being operated by thin metal handles on the handlebars.

Clutch?

"Uh, Ben. I don't know how to use a clutch, either", I said.

"Yer kidding…"

This was going to be one hard sell but Ben was up to the challenge. He musta wanted to sell that bike really, really badly. A quick trip over to Ben's house to see his motorcycle turned into an entire afternoon of crash-course motorcycle training. And I mean a 'crash' course, too.

After 15 or 20 minutes of instruction Ben declared I was ready for my first ride. Looking back on it now I can't believe I actually climbed onto that bike, but climb on, I did. I was a teenager. I didn't even consider I could get hurt doing this. I'd fallen from my bicycle many times and never got anything worse than a scraped knee. How different could this be? It's just a big bike, after all. Ben thought I could do it, and he'd convinced me, too.

"Now, when the engine catches, pull in the clutch and rev 'er up some to keep her from dying. We'll let 'er warm up a bit before you actually ride her."

Ben sure sounded confident. He was, after all, an older guy than I was. He had to be at least 20 years old. And he was a motorcyclist, so he had to know what he was talking about. I was as convinced as he was I could ride this motorcycle.

What happened next still astounds me today. I climbed atop the bike, put it into first gear, double checked the ignition and fuel were on and the engine was choked and told Ben, "I'm ready!"

Are you asking yourself the same question that escaped each of us that afternoon? The question seems so clear to me now, but neither Ben, nor I had the sense enough to think about it then. Remember that I'd never been on a motorcycle before. Ben was about to push me off into who knows what, atop a motorcycle I couldn't ride and one I didn't even own. I don't know who was dumber, Ben or I.

Ben was the only one of us who knew how to ride a motorcycle, but he was not the only one of us who could push one. That's right. If either of us had any sense, Ben would be astride the bike, and I'd be pushing him. That way he could start the bike, ride it a bit and warm it up some. Anyone who's ever had to push-start a motorcycle will tell you it's a tough thing to do. I think taking my first motorcycle ride on a motorcycle that was already running and warmed up may have been a bit easier than the shove into the unknown I was about to receive.

"It'll jerk some on ya' when it first catches. Don't let it scare you. Just pull in the clutch and rev her up when she starts."

"Let 'er rip!" I hollered.

And rip, she did.

Ben started with a mighty shove. The old Honda weighed a ton, in keeping with the way motorcycles were built back then. They were heavy and tough because they were built to handle any type of road. Ben was a lot stouter than he looked, and in no time he had me moving along at a good clip.

"Pop the clutch", he said when he figured we reached the right speed.

"Here goes!" I thought. I'd been keeping the clutch handle pinned against the handgrip but when Ben said to pop the clutch, I let it go with a forward thrust of all four fingers. The bike started bucking like a small pony, making rhythmic, baritone chugging sounds as it did. And it started slowing down rapidly. As hard as it was for Ben to push me, it got twice as hard once I let out the clutch and the engine started to turn. Just as I thought the bike was about to grind to a stop, something happened. The bike coughed loudly and began to pick up speed. In just a second or two I was yards ahead of Ben, who was jogging along behind me. The engine was running and I was riding!

Okay, I thought. The engine is cold. Ben said to rev it up a bit once it started to keep it from dying, so it'll warm up. Okay, the engine's running. Time to rev her up a bit. Forgetting to pull in the clutch, I commenced the 'rev her up a bit' part. I rotated the throttle what I thought was just a bit. It turned out to be a lot more than a bit. The eager little Japanese engine took in a big gulp of fuel and lurched forward so hard I completely lost my balance. My hands both lost their grip on the handlebars and I was thrown backwards. You guessed it; completely off the back of the seat and on my ass, in the street, with the motorcycle continuing down the road without me.

I had the wind knocked out of me for a second when I hit the ground. My first bounce was on my butt, and the second bounce landed me flat on my back, staring straight at the clear, blue afternoon California sky. I laid there for just a second, not really understanding what happened, and not yet realizing I wasn't breathing. I must have laid there for several seconds before I started gasping for air, just about the same time I saw Ben run by at full speed, chasing his motorcycle.

A few seconds after Ben ran by I sat up to see the bike slow down to a trot and begin to wobble from side to side. Ben managed to catch up to the thing just as it fell. Simple as that, my first ride was over. The bike ended up crashing, and I ended up sitting on my ass in the middle of the road.

What a rush!

I couldn't wait to get on again. I was hooked and I'd never get over it. I knew I'd buy that motorcycle from Ben, even if I had to push it all the way home (which wasn't far from what actually happened). I got up and reached Ben as he was picking up the bike.

"Doesn't look too bad. Couple scratches is all. "I don't think you hurt it much," said Ben.

Boy, was I relieved. I was quickly falling in love with this motorcycle, and I certainly didn't want anything to happen to it.

"Ready to go again?" Ben asked.

"Absolutely!" I said.

This time I pushed and Ben started the bike. He rode it up and down the street a couple of times, warming the engine up before declaring it fine and undamaged from my first ride. After a little more coaching I got back on and started practicing with the clutch. Learning the clutch was a pain in the ass because each time I killed the engine

Ben and I had the change places to re-start it. I didn't care and Ben, to his credit, was a very patient guy. For the next hour or so we rode the bike up and down the street, practicing my shifting, clutching, braking, starting and stopping. I was in heaven. I never had so much fun, and I didn't want it to end. I couldn't believe I was sitting there, atop this beat up old motorcycle, having the time of my life.

Ben finally stated I was ready to be a motorcyclist. He asked me what I thought, and I told him I loved the motorcycle and definitely wanted to buy it. I was having so much fun I almost forgot we hadn't talked business yet. I came right out and confessed to Ben that I only had $100 to spend on a motorcycle. I knew several guys who bought motorcycles for that much money or less. I was hoping Ben was willing to sell it for what I could afford to pay. As it turned out, he was. I think I probably could have got the bike for a bit less, but I didn't care. I saved up that $100, had it right there in my pocket and couldn't think of a single thing I'd rather spend it on.

After a little more than two or three hours I'd taken my first riding lesson, had my first motorcycle ride, my first motorcycle crash, made my first financial agreement and my first major purchase. This was definitely a milestone day. Over the next several decades, I'd make hundreds of these kinds of deals but this would always stand out as my first. I was proud of myself. I learned a new skill, made a new friend and, most importantly, bought my first vehicle.

When Ben and I finally finished the deal he asked if I wanted him to ride the bike home for me. No, I said, I wanted to do it. It wasn't very far and I could always come back later for my bicycle. I was ready for my first, true solo. Ben agreed to give me one last push and off I rode; no helmet, no eye protection, no gloves and no worries. And I did pretty well, too. At first.

About half way home, I stalled the clutch while trying to pull away from a stop sign. I knew I wouldn't be able to push start the bike myself. Even today I would think long and hard about push starting my own bike. It can be done and I've done it before. It means running alongside the bike until it's going fast enough, then jumping onto the seat, cowboy style, while simultaneously popping the clutch before the bike loses too much momentum. It's a real trick and not something I would have even considered that early in my motorcycling life.

I thought about walking back to Ben's house and asking him to push start me again, but I was a little too embarrassed for that. Besides,

I was just as close to my own house as Ben's. I decided just to push the motorcycle home. My very first solo motorcycle ride ended up in a mile long push. I didn't care. This was my motorcycle now, and I would have pushed it any distance to get it safely home.

I loved that motorcycle and cherished every minute I owned it. I knew nothing about owning and maintaining a motorcycle but knew I could teach myself anything I needed to know. I'm a resourceful guy and as good with my hands as anyone. Learning motorcycle mechanics was a snap. I bought a new battery for the bike, had a bungee cord rigged to the kickstand and was riding the motorcycle back and forth to school and to the store regularly in no time. I even removed the cracked side cover, took it to school, and had the crack welded by the seniors in the metal shop, using a special process for aluminum. Once the crack was repaired, the kick-starter worked again, and I didn't have to rely on the electric starter to start the bike. I liked this because I enjoyed kick starting the bike much more than using the electric starter. None of my friends with motorcycles had electric starters, and I didn't want to seem pretentious by using mine too much. Sounds goofy now but it seemed to make sense back then.

Mom and Dad weren't really all that happy about my motorcycle. I don't know if I misunderstood them, or if they thought I wouldn't really go through with it. Maybe it was the fact I brought the motorcycle home, out of the blue, without discussing it with them first. Whatever the reason, they weren't too happy with my motorcycle and put great restrictions on when I could ride it. I had to wear a helmet (even though we didn't have a mandatory helmet law in California yet). I could not ride the bike at all without first asking permission. I couldn't ride it at night. I couldn't ride it without a purpose, such as back and forth to school or work, and I couldn't, under any circumstances, take anyone for a ride. All of these restrictions were really fine with me. I got to keep my motorcycle and, even if they didn't let me ride it at all, just seeing it parked in the driveway each day made me happy. And besides, they couldn't keep track of me every minute of every day, could they? My brother and sisters all got super-secret rides on my motorcycle.

Speaking of helmets, I can only recall ever crashing the Super Hawk twice. Once was the very first time I rode it, ending up on my butt in front of Ben's house. The second time was about a month later. I was riding the bike home, pulling into the driveway when it happened. I always rode up the drive and past Dad's car to the very top of the drive. Once past Dad's car I pulled crossways in front of the car and left the bike safely at the top of the driveway. On this day, for one reason or another, I wasn't paying attention to the low branch on the tree that grew near the driveway.

I'd ridden under this branch a dozen times. It only stuck out from the trunk about 3 feet before it curved straight up, forming a right angled elbow that jutted out a bit over the edge of the drive. This short branch hadn't been any trouble before. If I came a bit too close to it as I drove up the drive, I simply ducked my head to avoid it. Almost every time. One day I forgot to duck and the branch caught me square in the forehead. Just like my first crash, I went backwards off the seat and landed squarely on my ass again, sitting upright in the driveway watching my motorcycle continue to the end of the drive and straight into the house.

It didn't seem like much of a crash to me, but it must have made a really loud sound inside the house because Mom came running outside within seconds. I had a large welt on my forehead, just below the forward lip of my helmet, and the wood siding on the house had a nice, black stained crack in it. After making sure I was okay, Mom lit into me for being so inattentive and careless. I think she may have even taken my riding privileges away for a while, too. In any event, it wasn't all that bad. The bike hardly got a scratch.

I thus began my life as a motorcycle owner. I'd own many, many more motorcycles over the next thirty-plus years but this was my first and as it turned out, one of the ones I'd own the longest. The motorcycles I actually owned the longest were my pair of TLR200s. I'll tell you about them later.

About 6 months after I bought the motorcycle I bought my first car. It was a Triumph convertible, and it was an awesome first car. I thought I'd end up forgetting about the Super Hawk, much like Ben had done, and leave it parked alongside the house covered in a tarp in favor of driving the car. As it turned out, I just couldn't bring myself to abandon the bike. I loved the bike and I loved riding it. It also was something of a chick-magnet where my beat-up old car definitely was not. I felt cool when I rode it and was convinced I looked even cooler than I felt. When it rained, or I had to carry something with me, I drove the car. When the weather was nice, as it almost always was in northern California, I rode the bike. The car and the bike both got used. I'd buy and sell 2 more cars over the next few years but kept the motorcycle.

I owned the Super Hawk for about three years before I finally sold it. We moved from California to the desert of Phoenix, and life was hard on my old Honda. Hondas built in the 1960s were definitely not the paragons of quality they've come to be known as today. While they were decent machines they definitely had their problems. One was a remarkably short life span.

One thing I learned growing up was what kind of service life one could expect from a vehicle. For a car, anything over 80,000 miles meant a car was on its last legs. It was rare for a car to reach 100,000 miles back then. For a motorcycle, the last-leg measure was about 25,000 miles. Why? I dunno. Maybe it was because most motorcycles were air-cooled, meaning they led very stressed lives, with the metals in their engines expanding and contracting wildly compared to a car. Maybe it was because they revved so high all the time. Motorcycles rev three or four times higher than a normal car engine.

I always looked at it like this: If engines were like hearts, and each is gifted with a finite number of beats, the one beating the fastest would wear out first.

Anyway, my poor Super Hawk, with over 25,000 miles on its clock, finally quit running. I took it to the local Honda shop where I got the bad news the engine was toast and needed a complete rebuild. Complete rebuilds were expensive. Used motorcycles were not. I made a deal on a newer model Honda right there at the shop. The shop owner was willing to give me a little something in trade for my Super Hawk, and I quickly became the owner of a lightly used Honda CB200.

I was really sorry to see the poor Super Hawk go. I was attached to that bike but the Arizona climate was hard on it, and I couldn't afford to have it fixed. I considered hanging onto it and repairing it one day when I could afford it. For one reason or another, I decided to part with her. She'd been a great bike (much better than the one I traded her for) and served me very well. I never regretted buying her, and she kindled a love for motorcycles in me that's never been extinguished.

The 650 Special

When I traded off the Super Hawk I ended up with a crummy Honda called a CB200. Built in the early 1970s, the CB line of bikes was awesome. Mostly. The first CB750s were the true super bikes of their time. CB550s, 400s and even CB350-fours were cool bikes. They had great styling, handled better and better with every passing model year and got more and more reliable as they evolved. The one poor bastard who seemed to get left behind was the CB200.

I owned that bike for almost two years. I wrecked it twice, went nearly 100 miles an hour for my first time on it and even took small trips with it. Even though I liked the bike, deep down, I knew it was a piece of junk, and I'd someday sell it.

In very early 1979 I started the Police Academy in Phoenix. Like most of my academy classmates, I'd given up a good paying job to pursue my dream of being a Policeman. In preparation for my drastic cut in pay I sold my car and had only the CB200. I moved from my expensive apartment, took a roommate, and lived very modestly. I was one of the fiscal exceptions, however. Everyone in the academy hadn't prepared this well.

While in the academy, I met and later became great friends with Tim, who, as it turned out, also liked motorcycles. Tim owned an almost brand new Yamaha 650 Special. That was one gorgeous bike, and I loved it from the time I first laid eyes on it. It was jet black, sleek, loaded with chrome and had a huge, powerful engine. It had such a modern look to it. It looked like it was going 90 when it was standing still!

I was embarrassed to tell Tim what I rode.

As luck would have it Tim hadn't prepared quite as well as I had for the poor pay of a Police recruit in the 1970s. We're paid relatively well today but back then we were starving. You really had to love the work to be a cop in the 1970s. Anyway, Tim couldn't afford the motorcycle payment anymore and was afraid he'd lose it to repossession. I couldn't let that happen. It was time for me to learn what the term 'take over payments' meant.

I knew I could sell the CB200 to some poor soul for around $500. Tim owed about three times that much to the credit union on the Special. I knew I'd come up short, even selling the CB200. I simply didn't have much money saved up.

"Just take over the payments", Tim suggested.

Tim and I went to his Credit Union and got the ball rolling. I enrolled as a member and filled out a credit application all in the same visit. This was not my first loan. I already paid off two car loans by then and think I actually had pretty good credit for a 20 year-old kid.

Wait. I thought you said you were in the Police Academy. What do you mean, '20 year old kid'?

Oh, I forgot to tell you. I was only 20 years old when I went into the academy. Actually, I was only 19 years old when the City of Phoenix hired me as a Police Recruit. Because the academy only started classes about every eight weeks, I turned 20 just before I went in.

Wait, I thought you had to be 21 to be a cop?

Yeah you do. Or you did. Well, anyway, since there was no Federal or State mandate (yet) on how old you had to be, the City of Phoenix decided to try lowering the age restriction a bit to 20 years old. The cities across the Southwest were growing very rapidly and so were their Police Departments. All these big cities were competing with each other for the precious few new recruits who were available. Most Police Departments had prohibitions against applicants who had used drugs and, to some extent, even Marijuana. They've relaxed these standards in recent decades (don't get me started) but, at least in the 70s, it was tough to find qualified people to be cops.

If an applicant ever used illegal drugs (except Marijuana) they were completely ineligible. If an applicant ever used Marijuana, there had to be at least a year's time elapsed between the last use and the time you became eligible for consideration. I'm not sure what you remember about the late 60s and the 70s but there definitely wasn't an abundance of qualified applicants. To counter this, they tried lowering the age limits to allow 19 and 20 year-olds to apply. They only did it for a year or two, and I was one of the only 20 year-old cops ever hired by the city. Ironically most people are corrupted long before they're 19. Lowering the age limit didn't help increase the available applicants much. It was a policy change doomed to a short life. I was a cop for a whole year before I was even old enough to buy my own handgun ammunition.

So, yeah, I was only 20 when I was in the academy. I was afraid someone would pull me out of a class one day, realize a mistake was made, and ask me to come back when I was old enough. Fortunately, that never happened. I graduated and have been a cop ever since. I know this doesn't have anything to do with motorcycles, but it's a neat story and I like telling it…

Anyway, back to the Yamaha 650 Special. After what seemed a long time I finally got a call from the Credit Union and was told my loan had been approved. I was the owner of Tim's beautiful motorcycle, and I could keep the CB200. I don't even think I had to put any money down. I qualified for a loan in the amount Tim owed and that, as they say, was that.

Cool. Now I had two motorcycles; a fantastic one, and a crummy one. It wasn't long before I sold the CB200 and had just the Special. Even though I put a lot of miles on that CB200 I wasn't very sorry to see it go. Not when I had a shiny, almost new machine like the Special.

And I loved that machine! It was the first truly fast bike I ever rode. In fact, it was probably the first fast anything I ever owned. I always got a charge out of motorcycling but this powerful new bike opened up a whole new world for me. Trips on the highway were no longer full throttle, white-knuckle affairs. I could go anywhere and ride as fast as I wanted to. This was the first motorcycle I actually took a real road trip on. A Gold Wing it wasn't but it had an all-day-long saddle and plenty of power for canyon carving and could rack up hundreds of interstate miles in a day.

Not that we had much of a freeway system in Phoenix in 1979. We had one highway that ran through town from north to south and connected Phoenix with Tucson and Flagstaff. It was narrow, old and always congested. Occasionally, you'd catch it just right on a Sunday morning and find yourself nearly alone. Perfect for a guy with a shiny 650 Special to see what she'd do. I made plenty of 110mph plus runs on this old trough of a freeway on the Special. I loved that bike and it taught me to love to ride fast. I've had many, many truly fast bikes since the Special but the Special was the one that got me started.

The fastest I've ever gone on this earth, without being in an aircraft, has been astride a motorcycle. And not a Police Motorcycle either. Police bikes are fast but they are far, far from the fastest bikes I've ever ridden. Almost every time I've traveled at a criminal velocity it's been aboard a motorcycle, riding like a hooligan.

Damn, I love that!

Anyway, I commuted back and forth to work, took weekend trips and ran errands all the time on the Special. I loved riding it and it was as close to a trouble-free machine as was ever made. In all the time I owned it, I can't remember anything ever breaking on it. It was perfect; dependable, beautiful, fast and just a joy to own.

Then I got married.

About 18 months after graduating from the academy, I met the girl of my dreams who later became the one, the only and the current Mrs. Overstake. She was quite a gal, and I knew very early on I'd ask her to marry me. She even took a nice day trip with me to Fountain Hills on the back of the Special while we dated. I don't think she enjoyed it, but we were in love, so she didn't complain too much.

In the years to come, she took a couple more trips with me on the back of a motorcycle but she never really cared much for it. We went on a trip to Tombstone, and the weather was miserable. It snowed on us in Tombstone, Arizona, for crying out loud. We took a trip to San Diego, and it rained on us all weekend. No, Mrs. O is definitely not a bike gal.

That being said, as newlyweds, she was never too excited about me riding the Special. She was always afraid I'd get in a wreck and be seriously injured. I tried to convince her that, as a seasoned rider, I was well prepared to deal with the dangers of motorcycling. As with anyone concerned about a loved one who rides, she wasn't as concerned about my riding abilities as she was about the morons I had to share the road with. She was right to be concerned of course. It can be murder out there in traffic on a bike. It's just something you learn to live with.

I would later transfer to the traffic unit on the PD, riding Police Motorcycles for a living. More about that later. One saying we had on

Motors was there were only two types of motorcyclists; those who
have crashed their bikes and those who are about to. More correctly
the saying is 'Those Who Have Been Down, And Those Who Will Go
Down'. And this adage always proves true. All motorcyclists crash.
It's the nature of motorcycling. It happens to all of us and after being
married for only about six months it happened to me.

I was riding to work one day in the awful Arizona summer heat
when it happened. I came up to the intersection of Southern Avenue
and Alma School Road, slowing to make a right turn. My light was
green, so I slowed to about 15 mph before making the turn. I didn't see
the pile of antifreeze some junk car belched onto the roadway just
before I got there. Slippery as snot, antifreeze is a terrible thing for a
motorcyclist to encounter. It doesn't reflect light like water does so it's
a bit hard to see, and it seems it's always spilled in the curb lane where
a cornering motorcyclist will hit it. And hit it, I did.

Boom! Down like a ton of bricks, right there and right then. No
warning. Just down on the ground and down hard. After sliding to a
stop, lying on my side on the 150-degree plus asphalt, I could only
think of one thing. What was I going to tell my wife?

I limped my banged up bike back home and walked in the front
door with filthy, ripped clothes and blood streaming down my road-
rashed arm.

For those who don't know what road rash is, it's best
described as having your skin run through a huge cheese grater,
then liberally coated with dirt, oil, grease, sand and gravel before
being ground again with the cheese grater. Ugly, painful and slow
to heal, almost all motorcycle crashes result in a road rash to some
degree. This case of road rash was a doozey and left scars I can
still see today.

That was the end of the 650 Special. No, the bike wasn't totaled.
In fact, the insurance fixed it as good as new just prior to me selling it.
It was my relationship with the Special that was totaled. My wife,
never fond of the idea of me riding, simply freaked out when she saw
me that afternoon after the wreck. I couldn't blame her. We were
newly married and loved each other so much. This type of thing was
very traumatizing. She knew this would happen, and even though it
was not as bad as it could have been it was bad enough. I promised my
wife I'd sell the Special and wouldn't ride a street bike again, unless
I was getting paid to do it.

Huh?

I always told my wife my goal on the PD was to be a Motor Officer. It was going to take a few years for me to build up enough seniority to get assigned to one of these elite Motor squads, but I never made it any secret that it was one of my goals. Even though she didn't like the idea of me riding a motorcycle, for some reason, she seemed a little more okay with the idea of me being a Motor. The day I crashed the Special I promised my wife I wouldn't ride on the street again (dirt biking has always been perceived as 'safer' than road riding) until I finally made it to Motors.

It was almost three years before I'd go to Motors, but I kept my promise. I owned a couple of off-road bikes in the meanwhile, but I stayed good to my promise not to ride on the street. The City of Phoenix owned the next real street bike I rode.

The TLR200s

About a year after I sold the Special I started to get the hankerin' to own another motorcycle. I really didn't want to ride on the street so much as I just wanted a bike. My best friend Harold and I loved to go out to the desert and ride dirt bikes on the weekends. We did it ever since we were kids, starting with mini bikes and later graduating to small displacement dirt bikes. We did it every chance we got but, sadly, it had been a long time since we had a chance to go riding.

Harold and I grew up together in Glendale, Arizona in the early 1960s. Both our families moved into the same subdivision when Harold and I were just 4 years old. We were neighbors. We went to grade school together and were inseparable, as good friends tend to be at that age. We played together every day, rode bicycles together everywhere we went and, generally, just grew up together

When we were old enough we got mini bikes we would ride in the empty lots around the neighborhood. If we were lucky, and could get Harold's Dad to give us a ride in the pickup, we'd take our bikes to the open desert. Oh, that was a blast. There's nothing more fun than getting dirty on a mini bike. And it seemed all of our friends had a mini bike or a go-cart to ride. There were some weekends where we'd have a dozen or more guys collected for hours upon hours of desert riding fun.

As we grew, so did our motorcycles. 50cc and 80cc bikes may not sound like much fun to you but to a 10 or 11 year old there's nothing better than graduating from a mini bike to a 50cc dirt bike. These were great fun and were as close to real motorcycles as most of us would ever ride. Except for Harold and I that is. For the next 30+ years Harold and I would get together as often as we could to ride motorcycles in the dirt.

Fast-forward some years. Harold and I are 13 or 14 years old and have been the best of friends for most of our lives. One day my Dad got a job transfer that would require us to move to San Jose, California. Even though I would come to love Northern California for the four short years we lived there, leaving Arizona was going to be a bummer. I lived in Arizona since I was four years old. I grew up in Arizona. All my friends were there and, worse yet, my best friend Harold was there. Moving was going to be traumatic.

I really enjoyed California. It was beautiful; so green and lush with so many things to see and do. And the weather? In a word, fantastic. I never realized a place existed where it could feel so good to be outside. We lived in California for about four years, and I really enjoyed being a motorcyclist there.

In 1975 my California life ended, and I found myself back in Arizona. Dad got another job transfer, this time to Mesa, Arizona, about thirty miles from our old neighborhood in Glendale.

I missed California of course, but it was good to be back in Arizona. I had a new town to explore and still had friends here I could visit. Most importantly I had a chance to spend time with my old friend Harold. I had a car and a motorcycle so getting around town was a snap. Harold had a car too so we got together often and always found something to do. One thing we did was resume dirt biking. Harold had a 100cc Suzuki dirt bike, and we had a couple other friends with bikes, too. We spent many weekends riding in dirt lots or out in the desert. Our favorite place to ride was in the desert north of Phoenix near a huge city park called Thunderbird Park. This area is full of new home subdivisions now but when we were kids it was nothing but acres and acres of open desert. We rode bikes, roasted hot dogs and occasionally drank beer we stole from our homes or paid someone to buy for us. Good times, indeed.

It wasn't long after moving back to Arizona Harold enlisted in the Army. He was seventeen and just decided one day he wanted to enlist. This was quite a shock because we talked about everything together, and we'd never even discussed the Army. Oh well, he was old enough to go and his mind was made up. He was about to embark on a career that would consume the next 20 years of his life.

Time to fast forward a bit again. Harold had been in the army for several years, and we didn't see much of him. Occasionally he'd come home on leave and we'd spend some time together but mostly we just corresponded with an occasional letter or postcard. I thought about Harold (or Hal as the now-grown-up Harold preferred to be called) from time to time. I was thinking about him the day I went shopping at Western Honda, in Scottsdale.

Western Honda was running one of their 'Huge Blowout Sale' ads in the Saturday paper. Since I was having the new motorcycle hankerin' I decided to go in and look around. I'm not exactly sure what I was looking for. My promise to my wife meant I wasn't looking for a street bike, and I didn't care much for dirt bike riding by myself, so I think I just went in to look around. That's when I saw the TLR200s.

Western Honda supported a program that taught young kids to ride motorcycles. They used an oddball motorcycle called a TLR200 that wasn't really a dirt bike and wasn't really a street bike. It was marketed as a trials bike, but it wasn't really a trials bike either. Although it had lights and turn signals and could be registered for the street, the TLR200 was small, light and not really well suited for street riding. Since it had the lights and stuff on it and a relatively small motor it wasn't really very well suited as a dirt bike. It has a slightly swayed back, like a trials bike, but it also had a seat and not very good ground clearance so it wasn't really a trials bike either. No, the TLR200, also known as the Honda Reflex, was definitely an odd bike. It was, however, well suited as a training bike for the riding schools operated by Western Honda.

When I was browsing around that day I spotted a small group of about five or six of these used TLR200s, straight from their duty as training bikes. Suddenly, I had an idea. Wouldn't it be cool to have a matching pair of motorcycles that could be used in the desert and on trails for Harold and I to ride when he came home on leave? I thought so. I got the attention of a salesman who told me about the bikes and, more importantly, told me they were priced very low because they were used and, well, to be honest, they were TLR200 Reflexes. They were not very good sellers, since they didn't really do anything very well. They were unpopular with the customers and, aside from being decent bikes to learn on, they really didn't have much of a market. He also told me this small group of bikes had been in their inventory for quite some time, and I was the first person who really showed any interest in them.

I didn't know how much a used Reflex was worth, but I knew how much money I had. I got the distinct feeling these bikes could be had at a very nice price, and I was right. I think the salesman began by quoting a price of $1295 for each one. When I told him I was interested in purchasing two he said he was sure we could work out something. Before long I was writing a check for two used Reflex motorcycles and making arrangements to have them delivered to the house. I didn't know it at the time, but I would end up owning these bikes for almost 10 years. They remain, to this day, the two vehicles I ever owned (and I've owned close to 200 vehicles in my time so far) for any long period of time. They would become a standby in my back yard.

They were perfect for what I wanted. When I bought them, I didn't get them registered for the street. I had that promise to keep and really never had any intention of riding them anywhere but in the dirt. I also never intended to use them as real desert bashers either so the small engines were fine. No, I simply wanted something that could be loaded easily into the truck, or onto a trailer, that would be dependable, easy to maintain and afford all-day-long saddle time spent exploring trails in Arizona. Yep, they were perfect.

And I can't remember anyone but Hal and I ever riding them. Hal came home on leave once or twice every year. Each time he did we got together to ride the Reflexes. Before he'd arrive, I'd make sure the carb jets were clean and the gasoline was fresh before strapping them into the truck or, later, onto the custom flatbed trailer I built just for them. I'd meet up with Hal, who, until we were in the car together, didn't have the slightest idea where we were going to ride. Sometime we'd go somewhere close, like the Aqua Fria riverbed or the area near Wickenburg. Other times we'd head north to the cool pines of Prescott or Payson, and sometimes we'd simply agree to a compass heading and start driving.

"Where to?" I'd ask.

"I don't care. Where do you wanna go?" would come the response.

"We haven't been south in a long time."

"I-10 or the SR-85?"

"Let's do the Ten this time."

"Let's do it."

And that's how a trip would start. We'd drive in the general direction of where we wanted to go and stop along the way to get water, maybe some chips or sandwiches for later, and maybe some soda if we remembered to bring an ice chest. We would drive for about an hour or two and find a good-looking place to pull off. We'd find an old farm road or power line access road and head off to spend the day exploring on the bikes.

We loved it and did the same routine every time we got the chance for many, many years. The bikes never failed us even though we'd inevitably drop them while we rode them. They always performed perfectly. When we got hot, or the bikes got hot, we'd stop and rest. When we got hungry we ate. When we got thirsty we drank and when it got dark, we'd load up all of our stuff and go home. We never got hurt, never got lost and never had anything less than a great time, every single time.

Except that one time of course.

It was late in 1991 as I recall and Hal was overseas mopping up after Operation Desert Storm. As a member of a scout group, he was one of the first US Soldiers to deploy to the Middle East, and he was going to be one of the last to come home. While most soldiers spent a year or less in this conflict, Hal was there for almost three years. During that time, I can only remember him coming home twice. Both were because of his Mom.

Hal's Mom, Ilse, was a nice lady who I knew almost all my life. I called her my Tante Ilse because she was German, she was like an aunt to me, and I think she got a kick out of it. While Hal was overseas she fell ill with lung cancer and Hal got permission to come home to see her. She wasn't too bad yet and after spending some time with her Hal and I decided to take a morning and go riding. With a sick Mom at home Hal wasn't willing to make it a long day but still wanted to go out for a few hours and get some riding in. You'd think someone who'd just spent a year in the Middle East wouldn't want anything to do with the desert but that wasn't why we rode. We did it because we enjoyed the riding and, more importantly, enjoyed spending time together exploring on the bikes.

It just so happened Tante Ilse still lived in far west Glendale and not too far from a small town called Morristown. Morristown is well known for only one thing; the Chrysler proving grounds are nearby. In the weeks before Hal's visit the news was lively with the upcoming release of the new Dodge Viper. The Viper was going to be the first, true sports car made by a US manufacturer since the Corvette. The motoring press was simply giddy over this car. The executives at Dodge and as rumor had it, Lee Iacocca himself were all planning an advanced, invitation only unveiling of one of the first pre-production Vipers at the proving grounds during the time Hal was home on leave.

"Where should we go?" Hal asked.

"It should be somewhere close." I said.

"How's Wickenburg sound? We could ride along the Hassayampa River."

"I know. How about Morristown?"

"Morristown? What the hell's in Morristown?"

"The Viper's supposed to be there, at the proving grounds. Maybe we can get a look at it through the fence."

"Let's go."

So we did. We drug the trailer with both bikes on it behind my little Mazda pickup out to the proving grounds. As expected, the actual road to the proving grounds was closed when we got there so we pulled off onto a dirt trail and found a good spot to unload the bikes. Before too long we were stopped along the proving ground's fence straining to see through the heavy brush on the other side to catch a glimpse of the Viper.

The Viper was a cool car, and we were excited for the chance to see one in person. This was as close as anyone we knew had actually come to see one, and we were a bit excited. We just couldn't see through all the foliage the proving ground had planted on the inside of their fence. We sure could hear the Viper though. The test car they were driving was loud. So loud we could hear the car (at least we assumed it was the Viper) haulin' ass on the track inside the compound.

We wanted a better look.

The only landmark visible to outside the fence was a huge, man-made mountain near the east end of the thousand-acre proving ground complex. This big hill had to be 200 feet high with steep sides to it and a paved ribbon of asphalt that went up and over the top. The top half of this hill could be seen for miles around, and occasionally you could catch a glimpse of a test vehicle climbing the impossibly steep hill, cresting at the top and plunging down the sheer drop on the other side.

We figured if we were along the fence on the east side of the complex, the side closest to the hill, we'd be in a good position to see the Viper if and when they drove it over the hill. Sounded simple enough. The terrain around the proving grounds was etched with dozens of little trails used by livestock or carved by men on horseback that were easily navigated on our Reflexes. Occasionally there were some old two-track roads used by property owners in the area. As luck would have it when we reached the southeast corner of the proving grounds, we found a small service road that ran north along the fence.

We decided to ride north along this small service road until we reached a point where we could see the hill clearly. Once there we'd find some shade, have a seat and wait for a glimpse of the Viper. As we started along this road the riding was easy. The trail was decent and clear and the bikes handled it without any problem at all. We even picked up the pace a bit because the trail was so easy to ride on.

I was in front and as was customary because of the dust we kicked up when we rode, Hal was about 200 feet behind me. As we wound our way along the trail it got a little rougher, a little narrower and a little more overgrown with brush. Suddenly, without any warning at all, the road simply disappeared from beneath me. I went over a small rise in what had been, until then, a relatively flat trail. On the other side of the rise, the road was gone. In its place, running perpendicular across the trail, was an arroyo about 8 feet deep and 25 feet wide.

Oh, shit.

No, really. 'Oh Shit' is what I almost always say, either out loud of to myself, just before I crash. I always have and surprisingly enough so do a lot of people I've talked to who have had similar things happen to them. It seems no matter how sudden and violent an event like this is there's always enough time for an 'Oh, Shit'.

I was only going about 15 or 20 miles per hour when I reached the arroyo. An arroyo, by the way, is a gouge cut in the earth by the sudden flash flood waters that are common in the Arizona desert immediately following one of the heavy rainstorms we get in the summer. The waters flow across the desert at a tremendous rate after these cloudbursts. Their rush across the desert floor is quite destructive and can carve these deep ruts that extend for miles. At such a low speed, my arroyo was too wide for me to jump. By the time I saw it, I was too close to it to stop. There was no choice. I was going into this abyss and there was nothing I could do to prevent it.

I had a split second to prepare for the inevitable. I twisted the throttle as hard as I could. With more speed there was a small chance I might be able to actually jump across this big booger. It was worth a try. I twisted the throttle and the tiny motor in the Reflex gave a huge wheeze as it tried to gulp in the sudden mixture of air, fuel vapor and dust. Unfortunately there just wasn't enough motorcycle, or enough room, for me to gain the speed required to jump this arroyo. With a huge pull on the handlebars to get the front tire up a bit, I flew off the near bank of the arroyo and straight into the thin air. I was now entirely in gravity's control.

Oh, I came so close. If the Arroyo was about 3 or 4 feet narrower I might have made it across. As it turned out, I was just a few feet short. Instead of landing on the opposite side of the arroyo, I hit the opposite bank with the bottom of the motorcycle. Bam! Back tire near the bottom of the arroyo, front tire near the top of the opposite bank, and the frame beneath the engine planted squarely in the soft dirt side of the bank. And I went from 20mph to Zero instantly. Well, the bike did at least. I actually kept going. My forward momentum carried me over the handlebars and onto the desert floor just beyond the opposite bank of the arroyo.

When I flew over the handlebars my death-grip on them tried to hold firm. I actually held onto the bars for a second as I went over and managed to pull the bike up the bank a bit before momentum finally ripped the bars from my hands. As light as the TLR200 was it was just too heavy for me to drag through the air with me on my flight. I landed about 15 feet beyond the arroyo and onto my right side with a mighty Whoomp! I had the wind knocked out of me, several of my right ribs broken and worst of all, my right collarbone broken. It didn't hurt too much at first. My baseball cap hadn't done much to protect my head (we never wore helmets when trail riding. Go figure...) and I was knocked out cold.

Later Hal told me from his vantagepoint it was as if I simply disappeared from the face of the earth. One second I was climbing a small rise just ahead of him and the next second I was gone. By the time he reached the arroyo he had plenty of warning there was something evil lurking on the other side of the rise. He stopped without any trouble. Once he did he saw me lying motionless in the dirt. He rode to a spot where he could cross the arroyo and arrived at my side in just seconds.

Hal said I mumbled a bit so he knew I was alive. He could also tell I needed medical attention, and fast. He knew I'd been knocked out, assumed I'd probably broken some bones, and decided he needed to go back and get some help. Hal moved me to a spot under a large creosote bush where I'd be in the shade and went back for the truck. He figured to fetch the truck, come back for me, and take me to nearby Del Webb hospital. Off he rode to get the truck, and there I sat, out cold, under a bush in the middle of the desert.

If the Viper really did come by it was probably during the time I was out. I didn't even get to see it.

After I laid there for a while I finally came to. At least a little. I was disoriented and in a lot of pain. I didn't remember exactly where I was, or what I was doing there, but I did know I was hurt, and I needed some help. I saw my bike lying on its side about 20 feet away from me. Even though I was confused, when I saw the bike I instantly knew what happened. I crashed on my bike and hurt myself. I wasn't quite sure where I was, but I could see a fence in the distance. Where there's a fence, there's likely some nearby civilization. If I followed the fence long enough I would probably find help.

I didn't remember Hal being with me, and I didn't remember him going off for the truck. For all I knew I was all alone and would have to fend for myself. I managed to get to my feet and took an assessment of my injuries. My ribs hurt. My collarbone was killing me, and my head was throbbing something fierce. In my condition, I wouldn't last very long on foot. I walked over to the motorcycle and, with a painful groan and a heave with my good arm, managed to stand it up and lean it against its kickstand. I walked around the bike and looked for damage. It looked okay to me. Nothing seemed too damaged or bent or broken, and it seemed if I could get it started, I might be able to ride it.

The Reflexes didn't have electric starters and had to be kick started. With my broken collarbone would I be able to not only straddle the bike, but start it too? Once started, did I have enough use of my right arm to ride it? There was only one way to find out and that was to go ahead and do it. I threw my right leg over the bike and thanks to its goofy, low slung design, I was standing astride it without any problem. Next came starting it. I checked the fuel and the ignition switch and once everything was ready I managed to give her several quick kicks. Thank goodness it was a small, low compression 4-stroke motor and kicked easily. Believe it or not she started and settled into a nice smooth idle. Damn, this was one tough bike.

Picking the bike up and starting the motor were a far cry from actually riding it. I had full use of my left arm and both legs but my right arm hung pretty uselessly at my side. If I were going to ride this bike I'd have to do it one-handed. The only problem here was my right hand was the one I needed to work the throttle. Without a throttle, I'd never be able to ride out and get help. After pondering this dilemma for a minute the answer came to me. Use the idle screw. I could bump the idle way up and feather the clutch enough to get moving. Once moving, I could lope along at a steady, if slow speed until I found help. But which way was help?

I had a choice. I could go north (away from Hal) or south (towards Hal). For whatever reason, I chose correctly and headed south. I'd hate to think what might have happened if I chose incorrectly. I wouldn't have been the first guy to die of exposure in the desert after becoming disoriented and wandering off in the wrong direction.

Anyway, I started my slow-speed rescue ride by finding a negotiable place to cross the arroyo and head south on the trail. As I rode, I began to recall what had happened. I don't know if it was the familiarity of the trail or if enough time had passed that some of the cloudiness was starting to clear from my head. Once I started to remember what was going on, I remembered Hal was coming for me. I decided to stop riding and wait for Hal. After riding for about 10 minutes, and almost reaching the southeast corner of the perimeter fence, I decided to stop, get off the bike and sit in the shade.

Hal was there in just a few minutes and more than a bit surprised to see me in a different place than where he'd left me. We talked for a minute about how I felt and whether we should leave in the truck and come back later for the bikes or would I be okay for as long as it would take Hal to load the bikes on the trailer.

"Load 'em up. I'll be okay." I said

"You sure?"

"Damned right. I don't care how badly it hurts. I'm not leaving my bikes out here!"

And that was that, for the Reflexes. Hal took me to the hospital where I got fantastic care for my injuries. Once at home he unloaded the bikes for me before my wife gave him a ride back to Tante Ilse's house. This gave me an hour or so to lie in bed, aching all over and woozy from pain meds, preparing for the lecture I knew would come when my wife got back. I remember how upset she got over the road rash from my 650 Special several years earlier. I was sure she'd explode at me when she got home.

As it turned out, she took it all pretty well. She mumbled something like 'boys will be boys'. She was more concerned that I was okay. I like that about her. Anyway, that was one of the last times Hal and I rode the Reflexes. When Tante Ilse died about five months later Hal came back for the funeral but riding the motorcycles wasn't even considered. After the funeral Hal didn't come home on leave as often, and I ended up selling the Reflexes.

Even though I'd go on to own more dirt bikes and ATVs in the coming years, nothing ever matched the fun we had on those bikes. They were fun, inexpensive, tough and dependable. For what we used them for, they were perfect.

Police Motorcycle Stories

I've been a policeman for a long, long time. I've had plenty of different jobs over all those years. Some were better jobs than others, and some jobs were harder than others. Being a motorcycle cop was both the best and the hardest job I ever had.

Motorcycling is tough, all by itself. There's a lot of physical activity involved in simply riding a motorcycle. Much different from driving a car, your body actually burns calories when you ride a motorcycle. Throw in some weather, such as 120 degree (in the shade) temperatures, freezing rain, hard blowing winds, blinding dust, hailstones the size of golf balls, glaring sunlight and disorienting pitch blackness, and you can see how hard motorcycling can be. Now imagine doing it while wearing 30 pounds of gear, atop a motorcycle loaded with equipment making it weigh nearly 700 pounds, in city traffic, for eight hours a day. Yes, you get the idea. Police motorcycling is the hardest motorcycling in the world.

And it's the best motorcycling too. If you're made of that kind of stuff, that is. The world is full of police officers that wouldn't ride a bike if you doubled their pay. There are others that think, as one of our assistant chiefs once said, all police motorcycles should be piled high in the center of Patriots Park, doused in gasoline and set afire. Police motorcycles are dangerous and the work is hard.

So why do officers choose to ride motorcycles? There are many reasons such as the dedication to protecting the motoring public or the extra freedom to roam the whole city without specific beat restrictions. Some Motors (as we're called) will expound on the advantage of being able to get around better and respond quickly to places where a regular patrol car can't go. Still others swear the demands of the job and the difficulty of the work make it a challenge they're eager to accept. These are all valid reasons for being a Motor, and we've all used them in answering the question of why we do it. Wanna know the real reason we all decided to go to Motors?

It's cool.

That's right. Even though we all come to appreciate the other reasons to be a Motor, the real reason we decided to get into this specialized line of work is because of the coolness factor. The uniforms are cool. The bikes are cool, haulin' ass everywhere you go is cool, and the freedom to ride almost anywhere in the city you want to go is cool too. Yep, we're all the same when it comes to being Motors. We all went because it was a cool job. Don't get me wrong, we're not all a bunch of vain fanatics. Well, okay, the vain part's probably true, but the fanatic part isn't. We are all dedicated to the work and wouldn't have become Motors if we didn't intend to do a great job. We had to be good, dedicated cops, or we wouldn't have successfully completed the competitive selection process. We were simply hard working cops that were lucky enough to earn a spot in one of the coolest assignments available.

Motors are a very fraternal bunch, too. When I meet other cops from around the country, and around the world, I can always relate somewhat to who they are and what they do. There are many differences in law enforcement from one agency to another. I have a pretty good idea what other officers do but when it comes to a fellow Motor I know exactly what they do. Motor officers are the same worldwide. Russian Motors do exactly the same job as Peruvian Motors or Chinese Motors or Canadian Motors or Montana Motors. When I meet a Motor from another jurisdiction I instantly know who they are, what they do and how they think. It's a very close and special fraternity of dedicated law enforcement officers who all share a certain degree of coolness.

I began my career as a Motor in May of 1985. I was a policeman for over six years before being chosen to be a Motor. The selection process was very tough and the competition for the few openings that existed each year was fierce. I had to wait until I'd been a cop for three years before I was even eligible. Once eligible I applied each year for three years before finally being selected and passing the admission tests and interviews. Being selected for Motors was just the beginning. Being selected and completing the training were two different things. The only thing my six years of waiting, passing the written test and oral exam earned me was an opportunity to attend Motor training. I wouldn't be a Motor until I completed three weeks of the toughest police training I ever took part in.

The training was very harsh. It was the most physically demanding training I've ever gone through. For the next three weeks, I would ride a big, heavy, beat up trainer for hours and hours on end until I was so tired I could barely move. I'd train in the heat until the physical exertion made me vomit, then I'd train some more. It started each morning at 4:30 a.m. and continued with precious few breaks until 1:00 in the afternoon. We worked these hours to avoid the high afternoon temperatures. The goal, after all, was to craft trainees into the most competent motorcyclists in the world, not to kill them.

Only about half of all Motor candidates successfully complete the training. The world has many police officers that couldn't make it through Motor training. And failing Motor training is nothing to be ashamed of. It's just that tough. When you leave your current assignment to attend Motor training, your position is not filled until after your graduation. Those who wash out of the training are welcomed back to their old posts with a knowing acceptance by their colleagues that the training is really hard to complete. So hard, as a matter of fact, the majority of trainees who wash out of Motor training do so because of injuries like torn muscles and broken bones. All this combines to make the successful completion of Motor school even that much more rewarding. A Motor officer definitely earns the right to become a member of the elite Motor officer fraternity.

I never worked so hard in my life. I dropped and picked up that trainer over 200 times during training. I scraped, cut and gouged just about every square inch of my face and forearms (which was the only skin not covered by protective gear). I strained muscles I didn't know I had. I ruined clothing with rips and stains. I wore out sets of protective padding, and I scraped a lot of paint and chrome off a city owned motorcycle. However, I made it and I was good at it. So good, in fact, I was invited back a year later to certify as a Motor instructor. Instructor school was every bit as hard as basic Motor training, but

I excelled at it and knew my tenure as an instructor would represent some of the most important police work I'd ever do.

I'm proud of every Motor Officer I trained. I often introduced myself to a fresh class of trainees as 'one of the world's best motorcyclists'. This statement wasn't entirely braggadocio. It was true and, more importantly, I believed it and vowed to all my trainees that, if they successfully completed the training, they would all believe it, too. I think you probably get the idea here. Police Motorcycle Officers are some of the best-trained officers and the most accomplished motorcyclists in the world.

Think about that next time you see a motorcycle cop.

Being one of the best motorcyclists in the world didn't keep me from being involved in accidents. I had several police motorcycle accidents during my Motor career. I'll tell you about some of them, too. What being a highly trained police motorcyclist allowed me to do was avoid countless situations that may have crashed an ordinary rider. I like to think for every time I wrecked a police bike, there were a thousand times my training prevented a wreck. That being said, I think I'll tell you about some of them.

The Fiesta Bowl Parade

In 1988 I traded my trusty old Kawasaki KZ1000P police motorcycle for a brand new Harley FXRP Pursuit Glide. Pursuit Glide sounds cool, doesn't it? Yeah, I thought so too and jumped at the chance to ride a Harley. Don't get me wrong. The Kawasaki is the best police bike ever made. The KZ1000P is the best combination of fast, comfortable, stable and forgiving when it comes to police work. The Europeans can rave about their BMWs and the guys in New England can brag about their Harley Road Glides but, for the rest of the world, nothing beats a Kawasaki. Kawasaki built these police bikes since the 1970s and the models built in the 1990s had evolved to the point where they were almost perfect. Aside from their tendency to snap clutch cables occasionally, you'd be hard pressed to find a Kawasaki rider that had anything bad to say about one.

That brings us to the Harley. As with most big city police departments, we had to have our vehicle specifications sent out for bids when we planned to buy replacements. Any motorcycle manufacturer who built a bike that met our predetermined design requirements could bid on the contract to supply our force with new motorcycles. The problem with this system is it led to occasional supplies of Moto Guzzis getting through. Oh, I can hear the Guzzi enthusiasts now. Get over it. Guzzi builds a nice bike. I just don't want to ride one hard all day.

In the early 1970s, the city re-wrote its police bike requirements making them very, very specific. In order to bid on the city contract for police motorcycles you had to offer a machine meeting these requirements. We wanted a bike having at least four cylinders, operated a chain final drive, was air cooled and weighed no more than about 500 pounds. In other words, as long as your company built a Kawasaki KZ1000P, you could bid on our contract. We found the bike we liked, and we wanted to make sure the other manufacturers didn't have a chance to saddle us with an inferior bike. Since Moto Guzzi and BMW made 2 cylinder, shaft drive bikes and Harleys weighed a ton, neither manufacturer could bid on our motorcycle contract. For many years, this guaranteed we always had Kawasakis to ride.

One year we got word we'd be getting some Harleys in for testing. We got three FXRP models that would be assigned to three different officers who would ride them for a year and submit periodic evaluations on their performance. Long story short, I volunteered to take part in the test and was chosen to ride one of the Harleys. In typical city/corporate fashion, it took almost a year for me to get my Harley. Finally, in 1988, I received a 1987 Harley FXRP to ride and evaluate. Our shop outfitted this snow-white bike with a radio, strobe lights, a siren and the Phoenix PD decals. It was a turnkey bike, ready to go, and I took to it right away.

One thing about the FXRP model was the way it looked. It was not the regular Harley that comes to mind when you form a mental picture of a Harley Davidson police motorcycle. Most Harley police bikes are built on what's commonly referred to as a 'Fat Boy' style motorcycle; so called because of the way they look. The Fat Boys are the stereotypical Harley; long, low, fat and slow. This wasn't what Harley sent me. Mine was a long, tall, slender bike Harley referred to as a Sport Glide. It was essentially a new model Police bike built by putting the biggest Harley engine inside a more slender Sportster style frame. I don't profess to be an expert on Harley's nomenclature so suffice it to say this Harley did not look like a normal Harley police bike. Which wasn't necessarily a bad thing.

I'd ridden several Fat Boys over the years. They are great bikes for all-day comfort. They have an excellent saddle and great riding ergonomics that allows a rider to work on them all day. What they are not is nimble. They are as slow and clumsy to ride as they look like they would be. They look great and they are comfortable, but they are also slow and cumbersome to ride. They are not well suited to big city Motor work. They're great for parades and such but, especially for running radar or responding to calls, there are better bikes. I think Harley realized this. What they needed was a quick bike that handled well if they were to be competitive with the Kawasaki. And they almost got it right with the FXRP.

The new FXRP was lighter than a Fat Boy was so it accelerated much better. It also sat higher and had better ground clearance so it maneuvered much better as well. A KZ1000P it wasn't but, if you absolutely had to work as a big city Motor cop on a Harley, the FXRP was as good a choice as you had. And I loved mine. Don't get me wrong. I recognized it instantly for its shortcomings and would come to miss my Kawasaki almost every day.

Damn it though, I loved to ride that Harley.

For one, it was a crowd pleaser. People really enjoyed seeing one of their Motor officers riding an American bike. I don't think a day went by when I didn't get thumbs up from someone who was pleased to see my motorcycle. Another thing I loved about the Harley was the sound it made. Nothing sounds quite like a Harley. The sound is rich, rhythmic, deep and powerful. I loved grabbing a big 'ol handful of throttle and hearing those big twin pipes bellow. There's really nothing like the sound of haulin' ass atop a Harley in full song. Nothing. It sure beat the whiny buzz of a Kawasaki.

Let's not forget about the saddle. If there's one thing Harley Davidson knows how to do it's build comfortable saddles. That Harley was one of the most comfortable riding bikes I ever had. I liked the seat on my Kawasaki. It was a good seat, and I could ride my Kawasaki for hours on end. I thought the Kawasaki was a very comfortable bike until I rode the Harley. Where the Kawasaki had a nice seat, the Harley had a comfortable saddle. I know that sounds like I'm splitting hairs, but the difference was startling. The Harley was really that much more comfortable to ride.

Okay, now that I've introduced you to the Harley, let me tell you about the only other advantage the Harley had over the Kawasaki. The Harley was built like a tank. It was bulletproof. You couldn't break one with a bazooka. I could drop that bike on the asphalt during training and not put a scratch on it. The super-sized crash bars were built of solid steel and were positioned perfectly to protect the body and critical parts of the motorcycle. They were so stout that dropping the bike in a parking lot wouldn't even scratch the chrome. Man, I loved that about the Harley. The crash bars on the Kawasaki, on the other hand, were tiny, hollow and bolted onto the bike almost as an afterthought. They were so malleable they could be bent by hand. When we dropped a Kawasaki, and the crash bars bent, we would simply brace a foot against the side of the bike, grab the bent bar and pull until it bent back into shape. Yep, Harleys were tougher than Kawasakis.

Nothing demonstrates how tough the Harley was then to tell the story of how I wrecked it. I'd crashed it a couple of times while training on it at the training track, but I'd only crashed it once on the street.

Every year the Fiesta Bowl Parade comes to town and every Motor in the city is assigned to work it. The closest thing we have in

Arizona to a Macys Thanksgiving Day Parade, the Fiesta Bowl Parade is a big, big deal. The planning for this event takes hundreds of people months and months, and it takes an army of participants, volunteers and police officers to pull it off. The route is long and runs for several miles along Central Avenue, right down the center of Phoenix. The parade precedes the annual Fiesta Bowl college football game by a day or two and people from all around the world come to see it. It has marching bands, mobile platforms for invited dignitaries and Fiesta Bowl officials and many, many parade floats.

Working the Fiesta Bowl Parade is a tough job and takes the coordinated effort of hundreds of officers, the most important of which are the Motors. All leaves are canceled during the Parade, and Motors work for two or three days straight to carry it off. We all had numerous assignments ranging from site security, to traffic control, to escort duties. We sometimes worked 2-3 consecutive 20-hour days, and it wasn't uncommon for us to sleep in our uniforms inside a command post mobile home, or on a couch at one of the stations, between assignments. This was one fast paced and detail driven event and we all did it together, year after year.

This would be my first Fiesta Bowl Parade atop my Harley, and the Harley would distinguish itself by performing flawlessly. One of the first jobs we had during parade duty was to escort the parade floats from their points of origin to their staging locations near the parade route. The parade normally started at Bethany Home Road and traveled south on Central. In preparation for the parade, we escorted the floats to side streets near the starting line where they were parked overnight while workers put finishing touches on them. These escorts could be short or long depending on where the float was located and what it was made of. A big, ponderous float, covered with thousands of flowers, could only go about 4-5 miles per hour so if it was built in a warehouse ten miles away it took hours to get it where it needed to go.

One thing we all had to battle with during these escorts was the overheating on our air-cooled engines and clutches. All of our bikes had motors that depended on the rushing air to keep them cool. If you're only going a few miles per hour the air doesn't rush much, and the engines overheat. When a KZ1000P overheats the clutch stops working. It simply locks up and the bike's engine stops when you slow down. The only thing that will remedy this situation is to cool off the engine. You can simply pull off and wait about a half hour for the metal to cool, or you can have someone give you a push-start and ride up and down the street for about 10 minutes, letting the rushing air cool the bike.

In this severe duty, the Harley never missed a beat. Sure, it got hot too, but the clutch was huge and never grabbed liked the Kawasakis and the engine was equipped with a huge oil cooler that, although the engine got really hot, kept it from completely overheating. While I watched my Kawasaki brethren fight with their bikes all night, I didn't have any trouble. I used the huge torque of the Harley, pushing against the back crash bar of the Kawasakis with my front tire, to push start them, one after another.

Truth be told, I took a lot of grief about my Harley. Cornbinder and Oilslinger were common names for my bike. I took it in the good-natured manner in which it was offered but there was substantially less grief coming my way on float escort night.

Once we were done with the overnight float escort we had about four or five hours off to catch some sleep or grab something to eat before we had to be at our fixed posts the next morning. Once the parade started, we each had to close our assigned streets until the parade passed, or sit at a 'hard closure' (one remaining closed throughout the day) until told to open it up. One by one, as the floats finished the parade, they were staged in one of the several parking lots near downtown. As Motor officers were freed up from their fixed posts they'd gather in groups of four or five and escort the floats back to where they were built.

The after-parade escorts were a lot faster than the pre-parade escorts. The parade was over, the float judging was done and the floats had served their purpose. They could now be stripped down and streamlined for traffic, and they could travel at higher speeds. We could get the floats back to their warehouses in a fraction of the time it took to get them to Central and Bethany Home Road the night before. This made the return escorts much more dangerous. There was more traffic on the road, and we were traveling at higher speeds. There was also the roadworthiness of the floats to consider. Designed to crawl along at only a couple of miles per hour, most of the floats didn't have any road safety equipment on them. Even though most were the size of a city bus, they were relatively lightweight, were mostly hollow and were powered by a scooter or ATV buried deep inside. This was okay at parade speed but could get hairy at street speeds.

This was the case when I was part of the escort team escorting one of the first floats home after the parade. Our float was a long, skinny thing made of chicken wire and chain link fence posts. Most of the ornamentation had been stripped from it, including the big 20-foot diameter globe that adorned the front during the parade. In the front of the float, sticking out like a jouster's lance, was a 25-foot long section of fence post. No biggy. We were all tired and no one considered how dangerous this could be. Tired as we were, we were conscious of this spike and we all made a mental note to be careful. And we were, almost all the way back.

There were four of us working the escort, and we were going as fast as we could with this float. We wanted to get done, get back for another assignment and get all these floats back so we could go home. On this escort, we were making pretty good time. The float was headed to the area of 51st Avenue and Camelback, which meant we could take Grand Avenue and save a little time. Grand Avenue is the old US-60 that connected Phoenix with Southern California in the old days. It ran along the old railroad tracks at an angle from downtown, northwest to Sun City and points beyond. Since it crossed major intersections at an angle it created large, complicated six sided intersections wherever it crossed the intersection of a N-S street and an E-W street. These 'Six Point' intersections could be tricky when doing a traffic break because an officer needed to be aware of traffic arriving at the intersection from all six directions.

No problem for a Motor cop. We simply took turns leap-frogging ahead of the group to the next intersection, blasting our lights and siren until all six directions came to a stop and sitting near the center of the intersection, making sure all traffic remained stopped, until the group passed. We did this over and over as we headed out of the downtown area towards 51st and Camelback. When we got to this intersection it was my turn to be the lead Motor. As we had a dozen times already, I lit-up with my siren wailing and when all the traffic stopped, rode into the middle of the intersection, turned off the siren and stopped. I sat astride my idling Harley, with every strobe light flashing, waiting for the float to come up from behind and go by.

I heard it coming. The little motor scooter inside was wound way up as it strained to drag the float along at about 20 miles per hour. From its sound, I could hear it as it slowed to make its turn onto westbound Camelback.

That's when I heard my buddy Abe shout, "Look out!"

I leaned left a bit and rotated at the waist in a partial right turn to get a look over my right shoulder at what was going on back there.

Just as I did, the skewer of a pole that stuck out of the front of the float struck me in the upper part of my right arm. The impact knocked me off balance, and I fell, along with the Harley. Within a second or two the float reached me and struck my rear tire as I went down. The float then climbed atop my Harley, with me still on it, as it laid flat on the ground on its left side.

So, you wanna talk about scary sights? How about lying on the ground, pinching the gas tank of your still-running Harley with both knees, while watching a parade float drive over you? I think I knew at that instant what it felt like to be road kill. I felt like a squirrel going under a Chevy. Furthermore, to make matters worse, when the float pilot realized what was happening, he slammed on the brakes and stopped with the float teetering atop my Harley and me.

Oh, Shit.

I sat beneath the float for a few seconds while my partners ran up to help. I remember looking up into the hollow interior of the float and seeing the scooter rider looking back down at me. I don't think I've ever seen such a shocked look. I can't imagine what was going through the mind of this poor bastard as he looked down past his sneakers to see the world's unhappiest Motor cop looking back up at him. I also remember thinking it should probably hurt a lot more than it did to have a Fiesta Bowl float on top of me. It must be adrenaline, I thought. The pain of all the broken bones and internal injuries probably wouldn't hit me until I was safely extracted from the wreckage.

Parade floats, for the most part, are not terribly heavy and my float proved no match for three pumped up big city Motor cops. Before I knew it they lifted the float and dragged me out from beneath it. I sat up on my butt and took inventory of my injuries.

"You okay?" one of the guys asked.

"My arm hurts."

"Where else are you hurt?"

"I dunno. Except for my arm, I think I'm okay."

And I was, too. Lucky to be astride my Harley, the bike protected me from the majority of the impact. The float climbed up onto the bike and the Harley's set of stout front and rear crash bars held firm. They didn't bend an inch and held the float up off the ground, keeping it from crushing me. As you can imagine I was certainly grateful to that bike. Knowing how malleable the Kawasaki crash bars were I don't think the outcome would have been the same if I'd been on my old KZ1000P.

My right arm hurt from getting smacked by the skewer but, since it was a glancing blow, the pole didn't penetrate much into the flesh. I had a bruised hip from hitting the ground but, aside from that, I was uninjured. I sure came out of this wreck well.

I got up, walked slowly to the curb, and sat watching the guys take measurements for the accident report before dragging my Harley away from the float and clearing the vehicles from the intersection so traffic could flow again. While the guys worked, the paramedics arrived to check me over and take me to the hospital. As they loaded me in the ambulance I hollered out to Abe.

"Hey, Abe!" I shouted.

"Yeah, man. How you doin?" Abe asked as he trotted up to the back of the ambulance.

"You know you saved my life, don't you?"

"That's what Ed was just tellin' me. Ed said if I hadn't warned you, that pole woulda hit you square in the back. You'da been skewered!"

"No shit! Man, I owe you."

"You'da done the same."

He was right. I would have. Any of us would have. From that day on I always had a special bond with Abe. I would introduce him as the guy who saved my life many, many times in years to come. I hate to think what might have happened if Abe hadn't hollered his warning when he did. If I hadn't leaned left a bit to get a look at the danger Abe was warning me about, that protruding pole would have run right through me.

Later, at the hospital, Ed and Abe came by to check on me. I'd already been x-rayed and was laying around waiting for the results. My arm felt a little better already. Ed told me when he spoke to the scooter rider he learned he had a blind spot inside the float he hadn't told us about. He could see out the sides of the float, and he could look at the ground at the painted lines on the road but he couldn't see directly out of the front of the float. He never saw me sitting in the intersection before he hit me.

Geeze.

The next thing I thought about was the nice insurance settlement I could look forward to as a result of being hit by a Fiesta Bowl float. I knew I'd get grief from the guys for years to come over being mounted by a parade float. A little compensation would sure be nice.

"Hey Ed, did that float have insurance on it?" I asked.

"You didn't see which float it was?" He asked.

"No. Why?"

"I think you'll like this."

"Okay. Shoot."

"It was the State Farm Insurance float that ran over you."

We didn't say 'Cha-Ching' back then, but this would have been a good time to coin that phrase. Between the actual owner of the float and the sponsor of the float, I would be well taken care of. They even paid to fix the damage on the Harley. I'm grateful to Harley for building such a strong bike. I'm grateful to those who wrote me compensation checks too and, above all, I'm grateful to Abe for saving my life.

Abe died a few years ago, at too young an age. It was a tragedy and I was as sad as anyone who knew him when he passed. I was also glad I was his friend. I miss him but I like to think as I re-tell the story of how he saved my life that he hears me, and he's smiling. Thanks again, Abe.

The Flower Boy

When I first went to Motors, I was assigned the swing shift on South Side. South Side wasn't the nicest part of town and even though things have improved some over the years the south side of Phoenix still isn't the place you'd choose to work if you had a choice. Still, I didn't care. I was a new Motor, and I would have patrolled inside a barrel if they asked me too. Besides, I worked several years on South Side already and even lived on the outskirts of South Side. I knew my way around and knew most of the officers there so I knew I'd be okay. I didn't plan on spending my whole career on South Side but at least for a while, South Side would be fine.

One advantage to working on South Side was the ability to go home for dinner. My wife is fantastic in the kitchen and can cook anything. She's as good at Creole as she is at Mexican and soul food. Home cooked dinners can be great at my house. If my wife cooks a big pot of gumbo, or a mess of enchiladas, there's no better food to be had. Why would I go to a Denny's for dinner when there's chicken frying on the stove at home? I spent a lot of dinner breaks sitting with my wife and little kids at my own dining room table. I was a new Motor, worked in an area I was familiar with and spent more evening time than most with my family. Life was pretty good.

One night I went home for dinner and enjoyed yet another meal with my family. After dinner, I simply had to walk outside, and I was back on duty. I decided to go down Baseline Road to find a nice place to run radar. There was a great place about 3 miles from home at 32nd Street and Baseline. There was a fine parking lot to sit in where I could have an unobstructed view for miles in each direction. After dinner, I got on the bike, lit a smoke and headed for Baseline. We weren't supposed to smoke on our bikes. The guys in patrol cars could smoke but the brass thought it looked bad for Motors, in full view of the public, to do it. It didn't stop us from smoking while we rode, it just made us smoke where the brass or the general public couldn't see us. Driving down Baseline Road, in the dark, I was unlikely to be seen.

I pulled out of the neighborhood and headed West on Baseline towards 32nd Street. It was a quiet night, and traffic was very light. I wasn't in a hurry and was just putting along when I noticed some movement off to my right. This section of Baseline was lined with several big, 100-acre flower groves on each side. These were long standing landmarks, and I always liked riding through the Baseline flower gardens because it smelled so good. The movement I saw was a dim light bobbing around about 100 feet off the roadway. It looked like someone was walking along carrying a small flashlight. It was about a quarter mile ahead of me, and I didn't really pay too much attention to it other than to note it seemed odd. Probably someone working the fields, I thought.

A few seconds after seeing the light it disappeared, and I forgot about it for the next several seconds. When I reached the area of the gardens where I'd first seen the light I saw a brief flash of movement and the same dim light I'd seen before. The movement was a bicyclist pedaling straight through the gardens riding between the rows of flowers. The bicyclist and I were on a collision course, but since I knew there was a shallow drainage ditch separating the road shoulder from the gardens, I knew the bicycle would have to turn before reaching the ditch. I figured the bicycle would ride along the row until it reached the end and, prior to reaching the ditch, turn right or left and ride alongside the ditch. Baseline Road didn't have sidewalks yet and there was a 6" tall cement curb separating the asphalt from the drainage ditch. Surely, the bicycle would turn when it reached the end of the rows of flowers.

What happened next was a shock. Just as the bicyclist reached the end of the flower rows he stood up and started cranking hard on the pedals. When he reached the ditch, with a mighty rearward pull on his handlebars, he got a little air from the ditch's bank and started flying. If I hadn't been saying "Oh, Shit!" to myself at the time, I might have said something more like "Nice Jump!" In true X-games style this little guy flew across the ditch, cleared the curb and landed with a perfect rear-tire-first landing, in the road, right in front of me.

The last thing I remember, just before I hit him, was the size of his eyes. They were so wide! Like an owl, he stared at me, illuminated by my motorcycle's headlight, realizing he was about to be hurt, and hurt bad. And he was right. He took the full force of my bike square in the left hip.

Boom! Down we went. I only laid down about 40 feet of rear wheel skid before the impact. At 45 miles an hour that means I had about a second to react before I hit him. There's no more sickening sound than the sound of the human body enduring a hard impact with a solid object. It sounds like a huge sack of potatoes dropped onto the driveway from the second story window. It's an unnerving sound but not quite as bad as the screeching and grinding of a motorcycle sliding on its side down an asphalt roadway. After hitting the cyclist I went down instantly on my left side. For the next 250 feet, I was a sliding mix of metal, rubber and flesh grinding along the pavement waiting to come to a stop. And the sparks! Damn, there were a lot of sparks.

My first impulse was to hang tightly onto the bike. I had a death-grip on the bars and had the gas tank pinched so tightly between my knees, I put dents in both sides of it. And I was riding it out pretty well, too. I could feel my left leg and left hip grinding into the blacktop, but as I slid, I fought to keep as much of my body as I could up off the street. The front and rear crash bars on the bike, even though they bent with the impact against the road, were still intact and creating a small pocket that kept some of my body elevated.

I slid at an angle down the road, across the yellow line into the oncoming lane before finally ending up on a section of dirt shoulder on the opposite side of the road. When I came to rest, I let go of the handlebars and let my upper body slump back onto the ground. My left leg was pinned against the engine's hot cylinders by the bent front crash bar. The impact pushed it back where it caught and wrapped around my calf, pinning it to the engine.

As I lay there, looking up at the starry night sky, I tried to take stock of how badly I was hurt. My left ass cheek hurt, my pinned and sizzling left calf hurt and my left shoulder hurt. Other than that

I thought I was okay. While I took this mental inventory, I smelled gasoline. Sure enough, the gas cap on the bike was leaking gasoline onto the inside of my left thigh. I might as well add a chemical burn to my injury list. Unless the gasoline gets ignited by my cigarette! Yes, it was still lit and still gripped tightly in my teeth. I figured it would probably be best if I tossed it, and I did (after taking one last, quick drag off it, of course).

Just as I flicked my smoke a safe distance away I heard the sound of an approaching vehicle. I thought it was a truck but since it was coming up behind me on westbound Baseline, I couldn't see it. I heard the truck come to a stop and then heard the patter of fast moving feet. Just a few seconds later a tall, skinny kid about 20 years old ran up to me.

"You okay, man?"

"I gotta get this bike off my leg." I said.

"I'll get it!" he shouted and before I had a chance to think he reached down with every ounce of adrenaline he could muster, grabbed the left handlebar and gave a mighty heave. His only thought was to get the bike off of me. He didn't know, and I hadn't a chance to tell him. My leg was pinned in the wreckage. The bike went up and over, taking my leg with it.

"Ahhhhhh. My leg's pinned!" I screamed as the momentum of the flying bike took my leg over with it.

While I laid there with my leg stretched out and twisted, the kid reached down with his bare hands, grabbed the bent and mangled crash bar and pulled it away from the engine far enough for my leg to pop free.

"You okay?" he asked again.

"Yeah, I'll be all right." I said, not wanting to tell the poor kid I thought his motorcycle barrel roll snapped a bone in my leg.

"Did you see the kid on the bike?"

"Yeah, he's over there, in the street. I think you killed him."

Now that I was free from the wreckage I could crawl in the dirt enough to see the kid lying in the road next to his bicycle motionless as death. The body was lying in the westbound lane, drenched in the high beams of my Good Samaritan's motor home headlamps. The Samaritan had been about a half-mile behind me when the accident happened. He stopped in the road to keep anyone from hitting the downed cyclist before running over to help me.

I managed to get into a seated position and stared mesmerized by the sight of the cyclist's body lying in the street. It looked like a pile of laundry, not like a person. Not really. There was a surreal look about it as if someone emptied a small clothes hamper in the street. Then, as the Samaritan and I watched, the pile began to move. Slowly, an arm rose skyward from the pile and stretched out, falling slowly into a horizontal position before the fingers of the hand extended. It was as if the pile were reaching for something just beyond its grasp. Then, with outstretched fingers, the kid grabbed at the asphalt and began to pull. He was trying to drag himself out of the road.

"My God! He's alive!" I shouted.

"No way!" the Samaritan replied.

"Go see what you can do for him. I'll call for help."

I reached for my portable radio as the Samaritan ran back to the downed cyclist. The old Motorola portable radios we carried were huge, about the size of a brick. I wore mine on the left side of my gun belt, opposite my gun. When I reached for it all I felt were jagged shards of plastic and metal where my radio used to be. The radio was shredded by the long slide on the asphalt that ground it down, exposing its now-ragged insides.

I drug myself back to the bike and, fortunately, the bike's main radio, protected from the accident by its high perch atop the handlebars, still worked.

"Tom 444." I barked into the radio.

"Tom 444, go ahead." Came the encouraging response from the dispatcher.

"Roll fire to 3600 East Baseline. I've been involved in a 962."

"You okay, Tom 444?"

"Negative, and there's a second victim as well."

"10-04 Tom 444. All units, be advised Tom 444's been involved in a 962 at 3600 East Baseline. All units responding switch to channel 4."

Within seconds, I could hear the sirens that indicated help was coming. An officer-down call always got a huge response. Any available officer would be on the way and the firefighters from the nearby Fire Station at 16th Street and Baseline would be on the way, too. All I could do now was lean back against the bike and wait for help. In less than five minutes cops and firemen surrounded me.

Everyone on my squad responded, in addition to several of the beat cops in the area. I waived the first responding fire unit away, directing them to the more badly injured cyclist. As bad as I hurt, I could wait for a few minutes for the inevitable second truck to arrive.

The firemen would routinely roll an ambulance (our fire department ran their own ambulances, equipped with paramedic trained firemen) and a truck. Since ambulances were significantly faster than the big fire trucks, they would arrive a minute or two sooner. The cyclist and I would both be in awfully good hands in just a very few minutes.

With so many Motors on site I knew the accident would get the best investigation possible. We were all highly trained investigators and our primary job was to investigate traffic accidents. It was a matter of pride to all of us to investigate as many motor vehicle accidents as we could. There were Motors on duty, over three overlapping shifts, from about 5:30 am until about 2:30 am the next day. With such good coverage, we investigated the vast majority of the wrecks that took place in Phoenix. Even back then Phoenix was a big, growing city, and we were all busy guys.

About 20 minutes after the accident, I was lying on a Gurney in the emergency room of the brand-new South Phoenix Ambulatory and Emergency Care Center. It would later be dedicated as the Jessie Owens Memorial Medical Center but when I laid there, it was still fondly referred to as the 'Space Center'. Mark was one of my good friends and one of my squad members who caught disposition on my accident. He showed up to the Space Center to do his post-accident follow up.

"How you doin?" he asked.

"Legs not broken, but I'm rashed up pretty good and sore all over".

"You're better off than the guy you hit. You messed that guy up!"

"Is he gonna make it?"

"Yeah, but he broke every bone in his body."

"Did you get a chance to talk to him, yet?"

"Yeah, a little bit."

"Did you get 'hold of his parents?"

"Why?"

"I thought he was just a kid."

"No, he's in his twenties. He's just a really little guy"

Mark continued to tell me what he learned. The cyclist worked for one of the big Baseline flower groves. He was out opening and closing irrigation gates in the fields on the North side of the road. When he finished, he headed back to the farm where he had a cot set up in one of the barns on the property. He'd been screwing around on his bicycle and said he never saw me coming until I hit him. Mark also told me the half-moon decorative visor I installed on my Kawasaki's headlight left a perfect half-moon shaped cut in the cyclists left ass cheek that was going to take about fifty stitches to close.

"I bet Sarge'll make you get rid of that visor when he sees these photos." Mark said.

"That's okay. I never really liked it that much. It rattled a lot."

We weren't really allowed to decorate our bikes. We were each permanently assigned our bikes and most of us even took them home with us at night. We took pride in their appearance and kept them clean and highly polished. Some of us even found little things we could do to customize our bikes. Some guys had pictures of their wife or kids taped to the tachometer face or would stick a Jack-In-The-Box ball on the antenna. One guy I rode with stuck a tiny rubber hot dog on his antenna and even another had professionally applied pinstripes added to his gas tank. Me, I had a chrome headlight visor.

About three months after the accident, I was sitting in my lawyer's office talking about the accident. Joe wasn't only an attorney. He was also a friend who I'd known for years. After the accident, I asked Joe to look into whether or not he thought I had a case against the cyclist's employer for an injury settlement. He said he'd look into it and, after doing some initial checking, Joe asked me to come to his office.

Joe told me the flower grower denied the cyclist worked for the farm. The owner even denied knowing the kid beyond the fact the kid's Mother worked there. Joe said without some proof the kid worked at the farm, there was probably not much we could do against the farm. The fact the kid told Mark he worked at the farm wouldn't be sufficient to proceed with a case. Joe suggested we needed something additional to show the kid worked at the farm. Since the kid was an undocumented worker, Joe was pretty sure there'd be no evidence on the farm's books about the kid.

I told Joe I lived near the farm and would go by in the next day or two to see what I could learn. As I drove home, I figured the kid, if he really did work on the farm, probably wasn't working in the fields while he recovered from his injuries. If I was his employer, I think I'd find the farm equivalent of a desk job for the kid while he healed. The farm operated a nice roadside shop where they sold flowers and souvenirs to tourists who would come to see the huge flower groves. It was open almost every day, and I thought there was a pretty good chance if the kid still worked on the farm, he'd have a job working in this shop.

It was worth a try, so I took my camera into the shop one day to pose as a tourist. I couldn't believe what I saw. If I remember correctly, the cyclist's name was Pablo. My plan was to come into the store and ask if I could talk to Pablo. As it turned out, I didn't need to.

I had no idea, beyond the fact he was a tiny fellow and was probably Hispanic, what Pablo looked like. That wasn't a problem. When I walked into the store, I saw Pablo, wearing a cast from his waist down, over by the coolers that held the fresh flowers. He was holding a large bunch of flowers in his hands and was standing on the blade of a two-wheeled handcart. While I watched, a co-worker gently leaned Pablo back on the handcart and wheeled him slowly to the back room.

The back room was separated from the store by a waist high wall allowing the customers to watch the floral arrangements being put together by the florists. Working side by side with two ladies on the florist's bench was Pablo. His co-worker parked him in front of the workbench between the ladies and left him to arrange the flowers he just retrieved from the cooler.

A saleslady asked if she could help me. In 'tourist' character I asked her if she minded very much if I took some pictures of the florists as they made their arrangements. She heard this request many times a day and assured me it would be okay.

"What happened to that poor fellow?" I asked, pointing to Pablo.

"He was in a bad accident. A Policeman ran over him."

"Oh that's too bad. I'm glad he can still work."

"Oh yes, he's been with us for years. Him and his momma both. That's his momma standing next to him."

Cool, I thought, as I began to take pictures of Pablo and his Mom making flower arrangements. They even mugged for my camera a bit, obviously used to having their pictures taken as they worked. After getting my pictures, I picked up a nice arrangement for my wife and drove straight to the Walgreen's to get my film developed. A few days later I gave Joe the photos along with a short description of my visit to the flower gardens. Needless to say, within a few months I got a modest settlement from the farm.

I felt sorry for the cyclist, and I'm glad he pulled through. In all my 30 years of police service, I've never killed anyone (I'm tapping the wood top of my desk as I type this), and I think the death of this poor farm worker would have haunted me for the rest of my life. The farm, however, I did not feel sorry for. Lying to Joe was inexcusable, although I understood it. The farmer couldn't admit Pablo, and illegal alien, worked for him on the farm. As it was he never really admitted Pablo worked for him. He did say, as the son of one of his employees, he'd simply been visiting his Mom the day I saw him in the store. Feeble as the story was, it didn't stop him from offering me a settlement to avoid the matter going to civil court.

I really am glad you pulled through, Pablo.

The Sick Lawyer

I've only been seriously injured a few times in my life and the worst that come to mind all happened on motorcycles. One of these motorcycle incidents caused me to meet one of the worst lawyers I ever met. Police officers, as a rule, aren't terribly fond of most attorneys. We have a terrible tendency to meet many members of that fine profession at their worst. In the world of law enforcement, we have several adversaries. Bad guys, civil activists, politicians, freemen, and anarchists can all give us fits. Among those that count among these less-than-complimentary groups are defense attorneys.

Don't get me wrong. I don't dislike all defense attorneys and have actually formed friendships with many of them. There are, however, some snakes in the profession who employ nasty tactics in defense of people who many consider to be the scum of the earth. If I live to be a hundred I'll never understand a lawyer who works hard to discredit an officer or, worse yet, an entire profession in the name of 'offering the best defense available' to a scumbag that needs very badly to be jailed, safely away from the public.

I've been shot at several times, stabbed at least once, kicked countless times and even beaten mercilessly about the head and shoulders on occasion. With all the altercations I've been in with bad guys over the years, the one person who came the closest to killing me, and maimed me in the process, was a defense attorney.

In the mid-1990s, I transferred to the South Zone DUI squad. I'd worked day shift, swing shift and a couple specialty squads while a Motor and I was ready for a change. The generally accepted rule of thumb when it came to assignments was to move around some during your career. About every three or four years, we liked to look for a new detail to work. This kept the job fresh and meant there was always another assignment to look forward to. This helped to keep you from getting stale or, in Police vernacular, 'burned out' in a particular assignment. Even though a lot of my friends found it easy to stay in the same job for decades at a time, most of us liked to move around a bit.

As a part of the DUI squad it seemed I was constantly on the move. We came in at 6:00pm and worked until at least 2:00am the following morning. We got to work in time to get hammered by the rush hour traffic calls, investigating accidents for the first several hours of our shift, then doing DUI patrol for the remainder. The DUI squad was the most demanding Motor job I ever had, and I loved it. Every night was busy and every night was different. Some nights we might work at a fixed checkpoint or be a part of a geographic saturation for DUI drivers. We worked in a different part of the city almost every night and were expected to respond at an instant's notice to anywhere we were needed.

Most nights were busy but one night in the summer of 1997 was particularly busy. We were working at the Central City Precinct, and we were getting slammed. For some reason, we spent the whole shift chasing wrecks and drunks. It was one of those non-stop nights that were so busy we'd lose track of time. Our Sergeant would check our radio status at the end of a night like this to make sure we knew it was time to consider going home for the morning. This was one of those nights. We were all running from call to call or processing drunk after drunk.

The night was so busy my partner Ed wore out his PBT. A PBT is a portable breath-testing device we all carried in order to give roadside breath tests to suspected drunk drivers. Although these devices would not yield results admissible in court, they were reliable enough for us to make decisions on the street, and we used them a lot. It was not unusual for a DUI Motor to use his PBT several times every night. For this reason, we had to make sure they were properly charged and had plenty of sterile mouthpieces in their kit before we went out each night. Even with the proper precautions there were nights when we simply wore out the battery or ran out of mouthpieces for our PBTs. On this night Ed already wore out his PBT and asked over the radio if there was another Motor that could assist him with their PBT.

Ed was at 24th Street and Thomas when he put out the call and, since I was at 52nd Street and Thomas, I volunteered to help him out. Traffic was heavy on Thomas, despite it being after 10:00 PM, and I was having trouble negotiating through the large groups of cars. Finally, at about 40th street, I worked my way to front of the cars and had a relatively clear road ahead. As I neared the signal at 36th Street it was red, and I started to slow down. About 100 feet before I reached the intersection the light turned green, and I hit the gas. I was at the intersection in seconds, and as I entered, I saw a flash and movement from my right. There was a car southbound on 36th Street that was not going to stop for the now-red southbound signal.

Oh, Shit!

The car, a late model (in 1997) Ford Taurus, ran the red light directly in front of me. I hadn't seen the car in time to react before the inevitable accident.

I have a deeply ingrained habit of 'reading' each intersection before I enter it. My 'Intersection Reading' class was one I taught at every basic Motor school and at every in-service Motor refresher. Simply put, I taught Motors to 'read' each intersection as they approached, specifically looking for any potential threat that could hurt them. Part of reading an intersection was looking up and down the intersecting street to ensure approaching traffic was reacting properly to their signal. In this case, had I been in a position to read this intersection properly, I would have seen the Taurus not slowing for his red light. I may have had time to react and maybe even avoid the accident.

Remember when I told you Phoenix was a fast growing town? In a way my accident was partly a result of this fast growth. Always listed as one of America's fastest growing cities, Phoenix was constantly expanding. Our city limits pushed farther and farther out each year until we rivaled Los Angeles in commute miles driven each day. In the 1970s most commuters lived within 10 miles of their place of business. By the mid-to-late 1990s, it wasn't unusual for commuters to drive 25-30 miles each way to get to work.

To accommodate this population explosion, new apartment complexes were popping up everywhere in town. Because the inner city itself was already so developed there were precious few areas where new single family homes could be built. To accommodate the people who didn't want to commute dozens of miles each way, apartments were very, very popular and could be built vertically on a relatively small parcel.

With population growth also comes traffic growth. All these new residents bring their cars along and every day these extra cars crowd the city streets. As the city grows, the streets need to grow, too. Well, you can't realistically build all the new roads you need, but you can do the best you can with the roads you have. This means widening the existing roads to accommodate the extra traffic. This could cause some problems with a street like Thomas Road.

Thomas Road was established a long time ago and was one of the original major arteries in the city. It was always a popular roadway and attracted residential and business construction along its entire length. Eventually, when it became necessary to widen it, the road would inevitably encroach on the existing structures. Buildings that used to have parking lots out front had to relocate their parking lots out back to allow for roadway expansion. When this happened the roadway could end up literally right outside their front doors.

This was what happened at 36th Street and Thomas. As the road was widened over the years it got closer and closer to the storefronts of its businesses. On the Northeast corner of 36th Street and Thomas was an old locksmith shop. This place was on the corner for as long as anyone could remember and in the old days used to have a nice little parking lot out front. By the time the summer of 1997 rolled around the road had been widened to the point where the shop's front door opened up directly onto the sidewalk that ran along the north curb of Thomas Road. The building was literally just a bit more than a sidewalk's width from the traveled portion of the roadway. Being positioned this close to the intersection, the building blocked my view of southbound 36th Street. Where I usually had a chance to look several hundred feet down the intersecting street in each direction, as I approached in this case I couldn't see far enough north on 36th Street to see if anything was coming.

I really didn't think about this at the time. I'm sure I made a subconscious note the intersection couldn't be read properly but, for whatever reason, I ignored it and simply plowed into the intersection relying on the presence of my green signal to protect me from the cross traffic.

Which lead me to meet a new defense attorney.

The Taurus appeared so quickly in front of me, I had almost no chance to react. I grabbed a handful of front brake and mashed on the rear brake with my right foot but realizing I was going to hit him at nearly 45 miles per hour, instinct took over, and I stood up in my seat. I teach my students to do anything possible to minimize their body's impact with a car. One thing I always taught was to elevate yourself high enough to clear the other vehicle if possible. I'd taught this theory a hundred times. Now I was going to get to try it out.

I was standing up when I hit the Taurus in its left rear tire. The force of the impact was immense, and as I flew over the car's trunk the

Taurus rotated in a counter-clockwise spin. As for me, I flew through the air about 40 feet before hitting the ground and sliding to a stop.

My helmet, although it did an excellent job protecting my head, was shattered from the impact with the ground. I was rashed up again, was sore just about all over and was convinced I lost my right foot. The pain in my foot was terrible, and I was certain it had been chopped off. Despite the pain and the hard impact, I was still conscious and aware I was lying in the middle of the road. All the cars I passed on Thomas Road would surely be bearing down on me any second, and I was afraid I'd get run over. As it turned out, I needn't have worried.

God loves Police Officers and nothing demonstrates this more than the reaction of four guys in a Chevy on the night of my accident. The first car to reach me was an old, beat-up Impala with four Mexican immigrants inside. Not usually prone to voluntary interaction with the Police, these immigrants didn't give a second thought to helping me. The accident occurred directly in front of them, and the driver immediately pulled his big boat of a car across two lanes of Westbound Thomas, effectively protecting me from the oncoming traffic. Later I would find, as a part of the completed accident report package, four handwritten Spanish witness statements; one from each of these good Samaritans. They remained on the scene, protecting me with their car and directing traffic until the first emergency units arrived.

After seeing the Chevy in the road, I could relax a bit and lay back facing another clear, starry central Phoenix sky. As I lay there I saw a middle aged man bend over me and look me in the face. He was dressed in a shirt and tie and was holding a police flashlight in one hand and a police portable radio in the other. He looked just like Richard, a friend of mine who I went through the academy with who was currently assigned to night detectives.

"Damn, Dick, am I glad to see you." I said.

"Hey buddy, relax. You'll be okay." He said.

"Did you call it in?" I asked.

"Helps on the way." he said.

I didn't wonder why Dick would be at my accident scene so quickly. I was just relieved he was there. I closed my eyes and listened to the reassuring sound of the approaching sirens. Within a few minutes paramedics and fellow officers surrounded me.

"Where are you hurt, officer?" the first paramedic asked.

"You mean besides my foot?" I said, believing the sight of a missing foot should have been pretty obvious to this trained medical professional.

"What's wrong with your foot?" he asked.

"It's chopped off!"

"No, it's not. I'm looking at both of 'em. They look okay."

"I'm tellin ya', my right foot feels like the front half of it's been chopped off."

"The boot's not even damaged. It looks fine."

"You asked me where I hurt. My foot's the worse."

"Okay, I'll take a look." he said as I felt him using the scissors to cut away my boot.

I could see his face as he removed my boot. The look on his face changed as I realized he was getting his first look at my now bare foot.

"You're right. There's a lot of damage here. Don't worry, we got you. It's badly damaged, but it's still attached." he said.

There were a couple of guys working on me, and they were busy cutting away sections of my uniform to get at the damage to my arms and legs. Just then one of the Motors on the scene asked me what happened. I told him briefly about the Taurus running the red light. He asked if I saw the driver.

"No, I never saw him. Talk to Dick, he's around here somewhere."

"Dick who?" he asked.

"Dick from night-dicks. He was the first one here."

"I don't see Dick around anywhere." He said.

I strained to look around and saw Dick standing on the sidewalk, about twenty feet away.

"There he is. In the tie." I said as I pointed to the fellow I thought was Dick.

The Motor I was talking to walked over to 'Dick' and began a conversation. I didn't think anymore about it, and before long I was in the ambulance on the way to Good Samaritan Hospital.

Good Sam, as we called it, had an excellent triage and they, as all hospitals do, gave fantastic care to injured officers. Within minutes of leaving the accident scene I was in a treatment room inside the ER getting the best care available anywhere. There were three or four attendants gathered around my foot discussing how in the world this could have happened. How could my foot have been so damaged and the boot I was wearing been so intact?

Despite how the damage occurred it was a bad injury, and it needed immediate attention. I'd have to see a surgeon soon but, for now at least, they'd stabilize me, treat the rest of my injuries and make me as comfortable as they could. A while later I was moved to another room inside a treatment pod waiting for my wife to arrive and answering questions from the Motors that were investigating the accident.

I later learned my Kawasaki was totaled. I'd never ride that trusty bike again. I also learned Dick was never at my accident scene. There was, however, a drunken defense attorney at the scene that bore a striking resemblance to my friend Dick the night detective. This drunken attorney also happened to be the driver of the Taurus, which explained how he happened to be on the scene so quickly. The flashlight and portable radio he was holding were mine. They'd been knocked off my gun belt in the accident, and he picked them up off the ground and actually used my radio to call for help. I also learned the attorney, named Vincent, denied he ran the red light. He told the investigating Motor officers he was southbound on 36th Street and had the green light. He said I was the one who ran the red light.

Fortunately, the Impala men stayed on the scene and were interviewed by the Motors. They submitted witness statements that all agreed the Taurus ran the red light. In addition to the men in the Impala, five additional witnesses came forward to say they saw the Taurus run the red light. Thank goodness for witnesses.

While I spoke to my fellow Motors, my wife and my doctor both came into the room.

"How are you feeling, Officer?" my doctor asked.

"Whatever you gave me in the ER is starting to work, Doc."

"How's your foot feel?"

"Still hurts like hell. It still feels chopped off." I said.

"You almost lost part of it." The doctor said.

What makes a tough old bastard cry when a loved one walks into the room in a situation like this? It's happened to me a couple of times. I'm as hard-boiled as anyone and a damned sight tougher than most. This still didn't keep back the tears when I saw my wife come into the room. Through the tears, I assured her I would be okay. I told her I was sore all over, but it wasn't anything that wouldn't heal. As it would turn out, I was a bit premature in this hospital bed diagnosis.

The doctor explained he wanted to remove the bandages from my right foot and take a good look at the injury. With my wife and a couple of Motors standing with him at the foot of the bed, he began to unwrap the bandages applied an hour before in the emergency room. As the doctor bent down to get a good close look at my foot, almost in unison my wife and the Motors slowly stood up and took a half step back. I could tell by the looks on their faces it looked as bad as it felt.

"Damn, Doc. What could have caused that?" one of the Motors asked.

"It looks like the impact broke many of the bones inside the foot, just ahead of the instep. The ragged edges of these broken bones penetrated the bottom of the foot at the same time. That's what caused all the tearing." He said.

He looked at me and said, "You must have been pushing hard against something with your foot at the time of impact."

"Yeah" I said, "the brake. I had my foot pressed hard on the brake when I hit. In fact, I was standing on it."

"That must be what caused it. When you hit, the impact bent the front half of your foot back so far the toes were pressed against the front of your shin. When that happened the bones couldn't take the stress and they all broke, ripping through the bottom of the foot and partially severing the front third. There's only some muscle and skin tissue holding the foot together."

"Can you fix it?" my wife asked.

"Sure." The doctor said, as matter-of-fact as if we were talking about a bunch of stubbed toes.

And that was that. I had some surgery later to stabilize my foot until a regular foot surgeon could take a more detailed stab at repairing the damage. A few days later I left the hospital with five knitting needles stuck in the tips of my toes. The surgeon opened up my foot and realigned the damaged bones. To hold them in place he drilled tiny holes through all the countless bones in there so he could run narrow needles through them. In a real shish kabob fashion, the surgeon aligned the bones along these needles, one for each toe, until he had five nicely aligned rows of toe bones. Once he finished, he sewed me up leaving the rounded-ball tip of each needle protruding from the tip of each toe. In a couple of months, he explained, the bones would be healed enough for the needles to be removed.

After the surgery, the doctor was very upbeat and his positive attitude was contagious. My wife and I were so relieved to hear how well the surgery went and were glad to hear the surgeon was particularly proud of what he could pull off. He even showed us pictures and x-rays he took during the surgery. He was right. My foot was a real work of surgical art and would never again look anything like it did that night in the ER. For the most part, at least, I'd regain most of the use of my foot. I could expect some loss of feeling and some limited range of motion but, especially when you consider how bad it could have been, I'd make a very good recovery.

I was out for twelve weeks after this accident. After the twelve weeks, I came back for a couple of weeks of desk duty before being allowed to go back on the street. I was another three or four weeks in a car before I finally got back on a bike. When I did I was welcomed back to the squad with a brand new 1997 Kawasaki. It was my first totally new bike since my Harley, almost 10 years earlier. All my other Kawasakis were hand-me-downs. This new one would last me until I retired from Motors about two years later.

So, what about Vincent the defense attorney? Well, to make a long story short, he's dead now. I only met him once, on the night of the accident. About 6 weeks after the accident, he fought his arrest in Phoenix Municipal Court and lost, of course. So many of the witnesses showed up for the trial the officers who investigated the accident hardly needed to offer any testimony. The lawyer, as it turned out, was in the advanced stages of HIV/AIDS and was in bad shape at the time of the trial. He chose to represent himself, and I heard he offered a feeble defense before being found guilty. My attorney friend would later tell me he only lived a few more weeks after the trial. Within two months of the day I met him Vincent was gone, and I never saw him again.

Want another example of how God loves Police Officers? Vincent had a shitload of insurance on that Taurus and about fifteen months after the accident I got almost all of it. By now we *were* using the term, 'Cha Ching'.

The RTX'es

It's always seemed motorcycle racing was more popular in Europe, and particularly in Britain, then in the United States. There have been times in Europe when the love of motorcycling bordered on hysterical. They own and ride motorcycles at a much higher per-capita rate than we do, and they attend motorcycle races by the tens of thousands. During the manic periods, they attend in the hundreds of thousands. Take the famed Isle of Man set of annual races, for example. Huge hordes of fans attend these racing events every year.

With Europe's love affair with the motorcycle comes the attendant boom in their motorcycle industry. There are so many motorcycles available in Europe it would take a month to count them all and a lifetime to see each one. Because of the European motorcycle mania, small manufacturers often get their start there. One of these small manufacturers was called RTX.

Never heard of an RTX? Join the crowd. Before I bought a ton of them, I'd never heard of them either. Don't worry. You're not missing much. There's a reason you and most of the world never heard of an RTX. They were pretty crude and never gained any real popularity before the whole business simply vanished.

The RTX was what we commonly refer to as a 'price point' machine. In other words, the RTX started life as a venture whose business model consisted of building the 'cheapest' motorcycle available. I wasn't there when the RTX Company got started, but I can imagine it started off something like this:

1st drunken Sot: "You know what we should do?"

2nd drunken Sot: "No mate, what?"

"We should build our own motorcycles."

"Why?"

"Cause Hondas are expensive."

"Yeah, but Hondas are nice."

"People don't care about nice. If we could build a cheaper bike, we'd sell a million of them."

"Barkeep! Another pint here!"

And there you go. At a bar, over a pint of nasty, warm British beer, a new motorcycle company was born. I owned more RTX motorcycles than almost any one man did, and I know them as well as anyone. There couldn't have been much more thought than that in the formation of the RTX Company.

Let me tell you a bit about the RTX. They were very simple machines built on the order of a motocross bike. They were lightweight, tall and narrow. They had only the most basic of controls and were very simply constructed. They were also, except for their frames, made from the cheapest materials available. The frames were a different story, and I'll talk about them in a minute.

Life for RTX started out as a marriage with a very little known motorcycle company from the former Soviet Union called Minsk. The Minsk Motorcycle Company was an old and very well established manufacturer from the old Communist Russia days. As with most of these state-run companies, they built a lot of different things and one of those things was motorcycles. As it was (and many say still is) the practice of Soviet manufacturing, their motorcycles were very crude, built with marginal raw materials using fifty year old technology. The Minsk motorcycles were terrible. And they sold millions of them. Remember, during the cold war a third of the world was communist. There were no Suzukis available to the poor citizens of these communist block countries. In fact, many of these poor motorcyclists didn't even know there was anything but communist motorcycles available.

Come to think of it, wouldn't that suck? Imagine how you'd feel if you had to choose your new motorcycle from a selection of only a handful of Russian or Chinese made motorcycles designed in the forties? Then imagine a 2-3 year waiting list to get one. Communist motorcyclists must have been a very frustrated bunch.

Anyway, after the fall of the Berlin wall and the opening of former communist populations to the free world it was pretty hard for these Russian and Chinese motorcycle manufacturers to compete. It didn't take them long to learn it was tough to sell their bikes in a free and open economy. This didn't stop them from trying of course. They flooded the markets with their wares that they could offer at prices substantially lower than the free-world manufacturers like Kawasaki and Yamaha. If their bikes could have been of better quality they may have succeeded but in just about no time at all their motorcycles quickly garnered the well-deserved reputation of being lousy bikes not worth their price, no matter how low.

Now lets fast-forward to the early 1990s. Our drunken buddies from the London pub want to build a new brand of inexpensive motorcycles. They are starting from scratch, as most of these small companies do, so they have to develop sources for their new machines. They have to locate sources for engines, transmissions, wheels, handlebars, controls and, essentially, every different part of the bike.

The big problem with trying to build a motorcycle using existing parts from established manufacturers is the cost. By the time you use a Honda engine and a Kawasaki front-end and mate them to a Ducati frame the cost of your parts is too great to make a profit. No, in order to keep costs down you have to figure out another way. Two options come to mind: build your own parts or find an inexpensive existing supplier. Alternatively, if you're a shrewd pair of guys like our pub patrons, you figure out a combination of both.

It was pretty easy to figure out these starving former-communist factories were having a very hard time surviving in the free world. It was a sound bet that a very good deal could be worked out with one of these factories to supply many of the parts necessary to build the new RTX motorcycles. Engines, transmissions, front ends, wheels and everything else necessary to build a motorcycle could be sourced from these factories for just pennies on the dollar when compared with mainstream manufacturers. Where an engine from BMW or Triumph might cost over $1000, an engine from Minsk may only cost $200.

The RTX guys weren't stupid. They knew if they built their motorcycles from all former-communist parts their machines would be perceived as poorly as the other former-communist machines and the new RTX motorcycles wouldn't sell any better than their Russian and Chinese counterparts. The RTX motorcycle needed to be different. It needed something to set it apart, while keeping the costs down.

One of the pub guys was actually a pretty good fabricator and had, on occasion, built some pretty decent motorcycle frames.

This seemed to be the obvious answer they were looking for. Use Russian parts in a nice, hand-made frame. This would keep the cost down and, at least a bit, distinguish the bike as being more than just a back-room hack made of crummy Commie parts. And that, in a nutshell, is pretty well what happened. The RTX Motorcycle and Leisure Company was born, building simple off-road motorcycles at a very attractive price.

Every RTX motorcycle began with a very nice, hand made frame built in-house at the RTX factory near London. This was actually a very well made frame and if the RTX Company only sold frames they might still be in business today. The steel used was top-notch and the fabrication was very well done. To top it all off, each finished frame was then completely chrome plated and polished to a brilliant shine. After the frame was finished all the Russian-source Minsk parts were installed. The result was essentially a Russian Minsk motorcycle with a shiny and very nicely made English frame.

The RTX was offered in two engine sizes; a 125cc and a 212cc. They were targeted to the beginning rider who wanted an off-road motorcycle on a tight budget. At this time in history a similarly sized Honda or Suzuki was selling for about $2500-$3000 while the RTX was offered at a very attractive $1595 to $1795, depending on the engine size. And at first they sold fairly well. As motorcycle-crazy as Europeans were, they ate up these inexpensive bikes, and the RTX factory sold bikes as fast as they could build them.

The first days of RTX were really pretty good. The bikes were selling. The parts supplies were proving fairly reliable and the bikes themselves were holding up well. This was really a bit of a wildcard for the initial years of the RTX motorcycle. The Minsk factory wasn't exactly well known for extensive research and development. They still built the crude stuff they'd been building for fifty years. They were also a former communist company and as such, not particularly in tune to customer service. It wasn't really known how well the Minsk motorcycle parts would hold up in the real world. They were, after all, designed as very basic transportation for poor communist workers and farmers to use on slow-speed back roads.

As it turned out, the motors supplied by Minsk were very robust. If one thing can be said about building the same thing over and over again for decades at a time it's that the bugs tend to get worked out after a while. Even though they were not very advanced, these Minsk motorcycle parts were, for the most part, pretty tough and were standing up well to their new role as off-road bikes in the hands of novice European riders.

So, if they were successful and were selling well, why aren't they still around? Why aren't there RTX motorcycles in garages all over the world? I believe it's called 'market saturation'. Eventually, every novice off-road rider on a budget who wanted an RTX finally had one. Even though there were plenty of these customers to keep the RTX Company going in the first couple of years, eventually these customers wanted to upgrade to bigger, better bikes. Unfortunately, there were no bigger or better bike parts to be had in the former Soviet Union. There was no evolution in the communist motorcycle industry. The poor RTX motorcycle was, sadly, a one-trick pony. There were no repeat customers because RTX had nothing new and/or different to offer them.

After their initial successes, the sales for RTX motorcycles began a steady decline and, eventually, there were sufficient used RTX bikes on the market to satisfy the ever-dwindling demand.

The RTX Company decided their customer base needed to expand. Their hope was to repeat their initial successes in new market areas. They decided to try marketing their motorcycles in Canada next. Before long, RTX motorcycles had a Canadian distributor and at least one dealership located in Eastern Canada. Despite their high hopes to duplicate their early European success, the RTX motorcycles simply didn't sell very well in Canada. Even with the Internet promising to extol the virtues of the RTX to a new, worldwide audience, they just never caught on in Canada.

Eventually, RTX motorcycles ceased production, and the pub guys moved on to other ventures. This would leave the poor Canadian distributor stuck with a bunch of unsold RTXs lying around. These leftover Canadian RTXs eventually found their way into the showrooms of a couple motorcycle dealers in the United States. There was one in California and another in Pennsylvania. The California dealer only offered these leftover RTXs for a short time before selling whatever he had left to the Pennsylvania dealer. The guy in Pennsylvania held on for a year or two, selling most of the last of the RTX motorcycles as a sideline to his lawn mower and go-kart business.

This is where I come in. Kinda.

During the first days of the Internet, I quickly fell in love with eBay. The Internet was fairly new, and I was, like everyone else, having a ball surfing the new 'net' in my spare time. As most of us new-to-the-Internet types, I liked to shop around on eBay. I never really bought much at first because buying stuff sight unseen didn't appeal to me. I simply liked to look.

One day I was looking at old motorcycle stuff on eBay when I spotted an odd auction for 'Pallets of Motorcycle Parts' offered for sale. The poor quality photos showed four or more pallets stacked high with boxes of parts, tires, wheels and frames. The pictures didn't offer much but the written description was very intriguing. It offered, in part, that this was the last remaining stock of the once thriving RTX Motorcycle Company. The description went on to promise the successful bidder enough parts in this offering to complete as many as fifteen of the 'famous' RTX motorcycles. Included in this lot were fifteen engines, fifteen frames and more than enough parts to complete fifteen new motorcycles. The parts were all new, never used and most were in their original packaging.

I was hooked and began an email string back and forth with the seller as the auction progressed. I don't remember what the starting bid on these pallets full of parts was, but I remember thinking it was way, way too much. As it turned out, anyone else who may have been watching the auction must have thought so, too. When the auction ended no one offered a single bid. In fact, I'd been the only guy who showed any real interest in the auction.

After the auction ended, Bill, the guy from Pennsylvania, and I talked in earnest about me buying these parts. Eventually, I agreed to pay $1500 for all the parts with my reasoning being I could build fifteen RTXs for about $100 each.

Boy, reading that last line back on this page sure sounds stupid.

As it turned out, it was. I should have known something was up when Bill enthusiastically agreed to my very first offer. He knew, of course, how much fifteen RTX motorcycles, in pieces on pallets, weighed. Long story short, after paying Bill $1500 and paying the shipper another $1300, I still had to arrange a place to store the pallets and rent a truck to pick them up from the freight terminal.

I don't think I ever came completely clean with my wife about just how much I really paid for the RTXs. Until she proofreads this chapter, I think she was under the impression I paid only $1500 for all of them. Well? Technically, that was true…

When the pallets finally arrived at the freight terminal in Phoenix my son and I rented a bobtail truck to pick them up. Junior was about twelve at the time and driving the big truck across town to pick up fifteen motorcycles was a real adventure. I rented a two-car garage sized storage space at a facility near the house and used this to store the pallets. My rental truck came with a pallet jack and a hydraulic lift gate so Junior and I had all the pallets unloaded and stacked in the storage unit in no time.

Once we returned the truck Junior and I went to work unloading and taking inventory of all the pallets. They'd been wrapped in plastic so each pallet was a great surprise as we unwrapped each one. We had a great time, and this turned out to be one of the best Father-Son projects ever.

Each pallet held wonderful treasures inside. One pallet had a collection of six upright crates, each containing a nearly complete RTX motorcycle. I imagined this was probably how these motorcycles were originally shipped from the RTX factory in England. There was a frame, with the engine/transmission already installed, a rear wheel attached and all the rest of the necessary parts for a complete assembly neatly stacked inside the crate. These crated bikes would only take four or five hours each to assemble into complete, running and riding RTX motorcycles.

Cool.

There were a couple more of these complete crated bikes on one of the other pallets and the rest were collections of smaller cardboard and wooden boxes containing hundreds and hundreds of motorcycle parts. One box had a bunch of wheel sets, and another had a bunch of engine/transmission assemblies. Among the other boxes stacked on the pallets were forks and handlebars and body parts and everything else you could imagine. Bill was true to his word. There were more than enough parts in this collection to build as many RTX motorcycles as one guy could possibly want.

I couldn't wait to get started and, about a year later, I couldn't wait to get finished.

Building motorcycles is hard work, especially when you're working in a storage unit. Every day was either too hot or too cold. I built RTXs in the blistering Arizona summer and the dreary, gray, if short, Arizona winter. There was one lonely electrical outlet in my storage unit that had to share the lighting, boom box and electric hand tool duties. Sometimes I'd treat myself to a portable fan.

I spent a little time almost every day for nearly a year building motorcycles. After I'd complete one, I'd test ride it, photograph it and list it for sale. I started off selling the RTXs locally using the Sunday paper and the Cycle Trader magazine. I had a hard time selling the bikes locally. They had absolutely no name recognition and they were not very impressive looking in a photograph.

I sold the first three in the Phoenix area but these were hard sells and took a week or two each. I figured if each bike took a week or more to build, and another week or two to sell, I'd be in the RTX business for much longer than I originally anticipated. At $90 a month for the storage unit I'd have over $1000 invested just in storage fees. I needed to speed the process up a bit.

Hello, eBay?

I decided to try selling the RTXs on eBay. I sold some things on eBay before but nothing on the scale of a full sized motorcycle. It would be a learning experience but all the rest of the RTXs I sold went on eBay. It sped up the process, too. I could start an eBay listing before the bike was finished and use photographs from the prior motorcycles since each one was nearly identical to the last. I had a complete set of photos for both the 125cc and the 212cc that only differed by their engine size. The only visible difference was the color of the engine; the 125 was painted black and the 212 was silver.

When all was said and done, I sold three in Phoenix and ten on eBay to people all over the country. I even delivered one to a fellow who lived near the airport in Flagstaff. The wife, kids and I made a picnic day of that one.

Of all the bikes I sold, I never got a complaint from a single buyer. They all held up well and made decent, inexpensive trail bikes for everyone who bought one from me.

Wait, you might ask. I thought you had fifteen bikes. How come you only sold thirteen? Did you keep a couple for yourself?

No. After nearly a year, I was sick of RTXs and the thought of keeping one for posterity never even crossed my mind. I took some pictures and that was enough memorabilia for me. As for the last two RTXs? They never made it to full assembly. As I built the bikes, I found a missing or damaged part here and there and decided early on I'd have to sacrifice one of the bikes as a parts bike to ensure I could assemble all the others. Near the end, bike number fourteen wouldn't start, and I found it had a bad stator in the ignition system. Since I used the stator from the donor bike already, old number fourteen would never be completely finished. At the end of my RTX run I sold bike number fourteen and the parts bike, along with all the leftover and duplicate parts, to a single buyer I'd met at the storage facility.

I'd become a bit of a celebrity at the storage facility. I was there so often I met several of the people who had stuff stored there. There were several afternoons when more than one 'neighbor' at the facility would chat with me as I worked. One of these guys showed an interest in the bikes and actually test rode several of them as I finished them. He once told me a story of being a Trials rider when he was younger. He was the only other person I ever met who actually heard of the RTX motorcycle. He spent some time in Britain as a teenager and recalled seeing them over there. When it came time to sell all the last RTX bits, including bike #14, he took them all off my hands.

And that was that. After a year of building RTXs in my spare time I was finally done. I built thirteen bikes that I sold for an average of $800 each. When I added up the original cost, plus shipping, truck rental and storage facility rental, I figured I made about $400 profit on each one. That sounded pretty good to me. I spent about 10 hours assembling, testing and delivering/shipping each bike. I like to think of it as a part-time job that paid me $40 an hour for about a year. Not bad, but not worth repeating.

When I think back on the RTXs I'm always glad I did it. If I'd known how hard it was going to be, I don't think I would have done it. The work was hard. The selling was hard and the time away from home was hard. If I had the room at home to do it, I might have thought differently of it but in all conscience I couldn't imagine putting my wife and kids through a year of RTX building at home. It was hard work but it was fun and a unique experience very few people can duplicate. Occasionally, when I tell the RTX story, I like to think I came oh so close to being the Arizona version of Paul Senior from American Chopper.

Sight Unseen Motorcycles

With the advent of the Internet, and eBay in particular, buying things without seeing them first became all the rage. I don't think, prior to the Internet, many folks ever considered buying a motor vehicle without seeing it first. In the old days, there were cars and motorcycles offered in department store catalogues and people in rural areas used to buy them. Things were different then. People trusted Sears, Montgomery Wards and JC Penney and knew the retailers would back up these purchases. Things are different today but the Internet can make people do crazy things.

One of these crazy things is buying stuff without seeing it first. Granted, a box of paper clips or a package of printer paper is probably an okay bet when bought over the Internet. Some other things, posted for sale with enough photographs, might be a safe bet too. It's hard to understand why someone would buy a big-ticket item like a motorcycle over the Internet. Even with plenty of high definition photos there's no way to know how a motorcycle runs, how it sounds and how it rides. It just seems, at least to someone with any sense at all, a motorcycle is too risky a purchase to be made on the Internet.

I've done it three times…

I couldn't help it. The Internet was new in the mid-to-late-nineties. It was cool and we all were hooked on it. For a motorcycle lover like me the Internet was full of possibilities. I could see pictures of bikes I could only dream of actually seeing in person. There were owners, riders and enthusiasts who posted things called Blogs, which opened an entire world of new information. Suddenly, the whole motorcycle world was at our fingertips, and all our motorcycle fantasies were obtainable, at least in electronically generated pictures and print.

It didn't take long to find out where the online motorcycle sellers were. All of a sudden, we had eBay and Cycletrader to surf through and, more and more each day, motorcycle dealers themselves opened web pages displaying their wares. When a motorcycle guy like me heard about a cool new bike the Internet was right there to offer pictures and stories to pique my interest.

Another cool advantage to the Internet was the new system of worldwide competition it created. Before the Internet, if someone yearned for a new Ducati, his or her only option was to shop at the local Ducati dealer. If they were lucky enough to even have a local Ducati dealer. After the Internet, a Ducati shopper could browse through a virtual world full of Ducati dealers.

If it was summertime in Salt Lake City and the local Ducati dealer had his prices appropriately high for the season a great price might be found at a dealer in Phoenix where it's almost impossible to sell a Ducati in 115-degree heat. Now a buyer could consider buying a cheap, one-way ticket to Phoenix where the savings on the new Ducati would more than offset the cost of the plane ticket.

Don't feel like flying into Phoenix? Buy a new Ducati over the Internet, have it shipped to Salt Lake City, and still save some money. Besides, it's a cool way to have an adventurous time buying a new bike. Suddenly buying a bike on the Internet was a real possibility. More and more people did it every day. On a new bike, it wasn't too great a risk, either. That's how I got started.

It was the late 1990s, and the Indian-made Royal Enfield motorcycles were being imported to the United States. They weren't very popular bikes yet and there was only a very small dealer network. I loved the idea of a new motorcycle that used fifty-year-old technology and cost a fraction of almost any other new motorcycle. The Royal Enfield Bullet 500 was the only model being imported to the states at the time and the closest dealer to me was in Oregon. That was just a bit too far for me to go to look at a new Bullet.

As time passed, I obsessed over the Bullet. I read every article and owner testimonial I could find. The bikes were sold for decades in the rest of the world, and the Internet was loaded with cool stories about the Bullet. I was hooked and decided I would find a way to buy one, even though I had to go to an out-of-state dealer to do it.

One day, while browsing motorcycle listings on eBay, I found a listing for a new Bullet offered by a small dealer in Nebraska. The listing was for a military model Bullet that meant it had olive drab paint, metal panniers and big, oversized crash bars. The listing included many detailed pictures, taken from every angle and in good light. It was almost like seeing it in person, and I immediately fell in love! It was winter and, of course, too cold in Nebraska to be selling many motorcycles. There was a great chance I'd be able to buy this bike cheap.

I watched the eBay auction for a week, logging on at least once every day as I tracked its progress. There were several bids on the bike but the price remained low until the very end. At the time, a Royal Enfield Bullet could be bought from a dealer for around $3500. I think the suggested retail price was around $3995 but most sold for a bit less. When this auction drew to a close the high bid was just over $2000, so I put in a bid of $2250. When the auction ended, I was the high bidder and won the auction.

Cool.

I emailed the seller and a day or so later, made arrangements to get a cashiers check to him. In the meantime, we spoke on the phone about arranging shipping for the bike from Nebraska to Arizona. As it turned out, I was in luck. The seller, who owned a lawn mower repair and equipment rental business (in the early days, just about anyone could be a Royal Enfield dealer...), had a friend who owned a trucking company specializing in transporting cars across the country. A few more phone calls and, for a very reasonable price, I booked transport for my new motorcycle as part of a load of cars going from the Midwest to the Pacific coast.

About 10 days after I bought the Bullet, I got a call from the truck driver arranging to drop the bike off the next day at around 2:00 in the afternoon. I took the afternoon off and waited for the truck to arrive. At just before two I heard the sound of air brakes hissing right outside the house. Sure enough, as promised, my Bullet was sitting at the back of the truck on the bottom row of a double-deck car hauler. It was covered in dirt and road grime from the long trip over winter weathered roads from Nebraska to my house but, despite the dirty appearance, the bike was beautiful! It was exactly as promised and delivered right on time.

It only took a few minutes to unload the bike and, after signing a bill of lading, the truck roared off, and I stood in the street next to my brand new Bullet. I turned on the key, the gas and the choke and, with just one or two kicks, the engine roared to life.

Nothing else sounds quite like a big bore, single cylinder bike. Thumpers or Lungers, as they're called, have a unique, rapid 'bump-bump-bump' sound to them. At idle you can hear every single time the spark plug fires and the Bullet, with its long, slender exhaust, had a distinct metallic sound, not too unlike a trumpet. What a blast! I threw a leg over the bike and took off down the road. I didn't even take time to wipe a clean spot on the seat for me to sit on. Wow, what a rush. I loved that bike and was pleasantly surprised at how very comfortable the ride was. The bike was slow but due to its rather hefty weight was plush and relaxed.

The Bullet was as old school as I hoped it would be. It was kick-start only, had bias ply tires and a four-speed transmission. It ran wonderfully and was fast enough to keep up with traffic, even on the freeway. It got a million stares every time I took it out, and people never tired of asking me about it.

Yes, I'd been very lucky my first time buying a bike sight unseen. The transaction went smoothly and without surprises. Believe me, in the years to come, I would find this was not always the case.

The Bullet was a very cool ride indeed, and I got many offers to buy it nearly every time I rode it. There were no Enfield dealers in Arizona yet. To this day, the only one I know of is in Prescott, about 100 miles north of Phoenix. The Bullet was a rare sight, and I often met someone who wanted one; especially the rather unusual military model I rode.

I eventually caved in one day and sold the Bullet to a co-worker that bothered me to sell it to him nearly every time we saw each other. After owning the Bullet for about nine months I finally sold it, at a small profit of course, to my friend. I didn't have much of an opportunity to miss the bike. At least not right away. I had my eye on a new Buell, but that's another story.

Victory

The next bike I bought, sight unseen, was a 2001 Victory V92C, full-dress cruiser. My good friend John lusted after a new Victory for months, shortly after they hit the market, and often spoke of buying one. One day he gave me his copy of 'The Victory Motorcycle: The Making of a New American Motorcycle', written by Michael Dapper and Lee Klancher. His well-worn copy of this paperback outlined the history of the Polaris Company's idea, from initial thoughts to final product, of developing a new motorcycle to compete directly with Harley Davidson.

This was one cool book, and soon I was just as nuts with the thought of owning a Victory as John was. A few months after lending me his Victory book, John bought a new Victory Sport from the one and only Victory dealer in town. That bike was awesome, fast and beautiful. When I got a chance to ride it, I couldn't wait to have one of my own. To make the bike even more appealing, my friend got a great deal on his, paying well over a thousand dollars less than the retail price.

Another company thinking they could compete with Harley Davidson was the 'new' Excelsior-Henderson Motorcycle Company. Excelsior-Henderson built a remarkable motorcycle; big, beautiful, powerful and very well received. Despite all they had going for them, poor 'E-H' went bankrupt after only a few years in business, and they were in their death throws at about the same time Victory was launching sales to the public. The Victory Motorcycle Company, needless to say, got off to a slow start.

With the memory of Excelsior-Henderson on the biking world's mind it's understandable that the buying public wasn't flocking to Victory's door. Many people thought the Excelsior-Henderson was a superior bike to the new Victory. If Excelsior-Henderson couldn't compete with Harley Davidson, what chance did Victory have?

Another strike against Victory was their shoddy initial dealer network. While some dealers sold the new Victory alongside established brands, like BMW, most did not. Most of the original Victory dealers were independent custom shops run by less than savory characters that built choppers.

Such was the case in Phoenix. The only dealer in town was a greasy, dirty old chopper shop on East Indian School Road. Not only was the shop in a lousy part of town, it was run by scary looking typical biker types. I was with my friend the day he bought his new Sport model. As enamored as he was with the bike, I think he almost walked out when he saw the shop. Not only was this ugly shop the only place in town to buy one, it was also the only place in town to honor the warranty.

After John rode his Victory Sport for several months I learned how unimportant the warrantee really was. John's bike was proving to be very nice, very tough and, above all, very reliable. John rode his very hard too. The Victory was one well-built motorcycle, and I wanted one more than ever.

One day I spotted an ad for Victory motorcycles offered by 'The Newest Victory Dealer in the Southwest'. Unfortunately, this new dealer wasn't in Phoenix, or even in Arizona. This new dealer was in Henderson, Nevada. This wasn't all that bad, as Henderson is only about 300 miles from Phoenix and a leisurely five-hour drive, over the Hoover Dam, on the road to Vegas. This new dealer made a name in the Vegas area by selling high-end customs like Big Dog, Confederate and Boss Hoss motorcycles and now carried Victory Motorcycles. They had a cool web site that offered all sorts of info on their shop, their bikes and their 'outstanding' service and sales departments. They also offered drastic discounts on the price of new Victories along with special finance rates.

After reading their ad and surfing their web site, I was on the phone to one of the shop's owners, who was also a salesman. Before I knew it I made a deal for a new, full dressed Victory V92C. I bought it for thousands less than the MSRP and got crazy low financing on it. They were very eager to get some of these new Victories onto the highway.

A few days later I was on the road to Henderson driving my wife's new F-150 with a ramp and some tie-downs bouncing around in the bed. I left at around 6:00AM and was back, having Junior and Mrs. O help me unload that monster from the back of the truck, before dinnertime.

When I pulled up to the dealer I was more than just a bit disappointed. The photographs on their web site depicted a new, state of the art dealership. The big, bright and shiny dealership shown in the web site photos was, in reality, an old converted gas station. In the middle of the parking lot was a raised concrete island with protruding rusted bolts, sticking up at bent angles, that one time held gas pumps. The shop was covered on one side with local gang graffiti and on another side with crudely drawn representations of the Harley logo. The dealer was next door to an even older automotive garage, littered with broken down cars and a stereotypical 55 gallon drum full of burning scraps of wood that kept a couple of mechanics warm as they drank coffee and smoked cigarettes.

Geeze...

It would be many more years before Victory motorcycles established a reliable network of real-world dealers. In the beginning, they apparently took what they could get. In all fairness to my 'Newest Victory Dealer in the Southwest', what money they invested into their dealership was all spent indoors. The showroom was nice, bright and clean. The floor was covered in dozen or more very expensive custom motorcycles, which cost several times what I was about to pay for my Victory. They were also very well organized there, too. As promised, all the paperwork was done, and the bike was cleaned, prepped and ready to go. In less than an hour I signed on each dotted line, took a quick test ride around the block and watched as several guys loaded my new bike into the back of the truck. I was so excited to get my new bike home. I didn't even stop at a casino while in town.

I never really fell deeply in love with my new Victory. It just never grew on me. It wasn't that there was anything really wrong with the bike. I think it was more that there wasn't anything really right with the bike. It wasn't outstanding at anything it did. The styling wasn't very original, and it was constantly being mistaken for just another Harley. It wasn't any more powerful than a Harley, and it rode very much like a Harley. I don't think there's anything really wrong with that, but it seemed that Victory wanted so much to compete with Harley that they ended up with a motorcycle that was very much just like a Harley. In the beginning at least, Victory was so much like Harley that the only real reason to buy one was because they could be purchased at a price thousands of dollars less than a Harley. I don't think that a bike just as good as a Harley but at a better price was what Victory was supposed to be all about.

The first generation Victory motorcycles were a bit crude. They had rough, rather angular styling that never really caught on very well. The engines, although very powerful and robust, were noisy, clunky and had an industrial look. In years to come the Victory would evolve into a beautiful machine that successfully addressed every issue the original models had. While the original Victory looked as if it had agricultural roots, the new models have the look of very expensive, hand made custom bikes. The new bikes are extremely well refined and are finally recognized as true alternatives to the Harley instead of just another Harley copy.

If Victory hadn't been backed by the immense size of their parent company, Polaris, they may have very likely gone the way of the Excelsior-Henderson. Fortunately, they stuck with their product, made improvements year after year, and invested in their ideas even when they weren't making any money.

Good for Victory.

Capo

The third bike I bought, sight unseen, was an Aprilia Caponord. It was shortly after I sold the Victory, and I was longing for something fast. Even though I'm not getting any younger, I still get the yearning to ride really, really fast. I call it my 'hankerin to haul ass'. I'd been through it a couple of times before and this time I had it bad. I was thinking about a Ducati 996 or maybe one of the newly designed Moto Guzzi Brevas. Maybe even a Japanese Liter-Bike would do. I just wanted a bike I could lay wide open and scorch the earth with.

I was watching a motorcycle Gran Prix on cable one day when I noticed Aprilia seemed to always have a bike on the leader board. I never really paid much attention to Aprilia. I thought they were high-end bikes, like Benellis, that were made in limited numbers and were very, very expensive. It may have been that way at one time but around 2003, they expanded their line and offered several reasonably priced bikes.

Aprilia wasn't just a race bike company. They actually owned Moto Guzzi and Laverda and were in the process of merging with scooter giant Piaggio. They had a new Liter-Class bike, called a Tuono, which really looked cool and would definitely fit the bill as a haul-ass machine. However, they were a bit pricey, so I never really seriously considered them. Even though they weren't as expensive as

I'd originally thought they were substantially more expensive than their Japanese counterparts.

One day, in the dead of winter, I was reading a story about the worst blizzard to hit Denver in decades. The snow was so heavy and came on so quickly it literally had the city paralyzed. There were many closed roads. Businesses were closed. Schools were closed and the storms caused many hundreds of thousands of dollars in damage. In one of the Denver blizzard stories was a sidebar about a motorcycle dealership whose roof had collapsed under the weight of the snow. There were dozens of motorcycles damaged or destroyed in this unfortunate incident and the photo accompanying the story showed the storefront, barely recognizable as a motorcycle dealer. The one thing recognizable in the photo was an Aprilia motorcycle banner.

I wonder…

I looked up the web page for the dealer named in the Denver blizzard story. I remember it was a Saturday when I read the story. I made a mental note to recheck the web page in a few days. Maybe, just maybe, they'd be having a Snow Sale!

I waited until the following Tuesday before checking their web page. I figured most motorcycle dealers were closed on Sunday and Monday, and if they were going to reopen at all, the soonest would be the following Tuesday. I logged onto their web page and there were no changes. I'm not sure what I was hoping for but, even in the online world, it takes time to recover from a collapsed roof after a record setting blizzard. I decided to call on the phone and got a message asking customers to be patient, to give them a few days, and they hoped to have their office staff available.

About a week later I was surfing eBay, looking at motorcycles and Aprlias in particular. I spotted several recent listings originating from a dealer in the Denver area. It had to be the same one, didn't it? Of course it did. I called the dealer in Denver and learned that, yes, they were listing several motorcycles on eBay while they waited for repairs to be made to their shop. The salesman was very nice and, even as hectic as his life had to be at the time, took the time to talk Aprilia with me. As the result of that conversation I was convinced that an Aprilia Caponord was the bike for me.

The Caponord was an odd bike compared to the other Aprilia offerings. It was an upright motorcycle, a bit like a dual-purpose bike, but with street tires on it. It was nothing like the Tuono or the Mille models that were definite sport bikes, bred from racing. The Caponord looked like a cross between a race bike and a tour bike. This comfortable, upright riding position, combined with the same hundred-horsepower engine as their sport bikes, made the Caponord very compelling. Not only did this bike look comfortable, it was also guaranteed to haul some very serious ass!

I ended up buying the Caponord offered on eBay for a very good price and after about a week was unpacking it in the driveway. It arrived via freight truck and was packaged in a custom made crate. It was fully assembled, prepped by the dealer, and was ready to ride, right out of the box. And it was cool, too.

The Caponord was as fast as I hoped. It was easily capable of very high speeds and could cruise at triple digits for long periods without compliant. And I did just that, every chance I got. I loved riding that bike fast. As with all my bikes I rode it often, enjoyed it immensely, and sold it after about a year. If you ever get the hankerin' to haul some serious ass, and like to ride in a comfortable, upright seat, the Caponord is perfect.

Nearly Famous on a Police Bike

Being a motorcycle cop, I had many opportunities to brush shoulders with famous people. Every time a big political figure came to town all the city's Motor cops were mobilized to provide escort and security duty for them. The highest profile of these were heads of state and, most importantly, The President of the United States. I rode Motors for the better part of 15 years from the mid-eighties until the end of the nineties. As Phoenix is a popular place for vacationing and campaigning, I met a lot of politicians, and every president we had, while I was a Motor.

I mean it when I said 'met'. Not only did I ride escort duty for all of them, I actually got to meet them too. Everyone sees the presidential motorcades on television, surrounded by local motorcops as they roar around town tying up traffic for miles. One thing you don't see is what happens at the end of these escorts. After the motorcade disappears past all the security, and away from the prying eyes of the public, there's always a chance to pause and catch our collective breaths. When we do, the dignitary we escort almost always takes a few minutes to thank the group of motorcops that escorted them. In the case of the President, there is a member of the White House Staff that takes some individual and group photos. These photos always manage to find their way to us, and we all have a small collection of handshaking and group-hug type photos in a folder in a desk drawer somewhere.

Escorting a dignitary is very hard work. The pressure to get there quickly and safely is tremendous. This is high-level, heart pounding work done with a massive amount of adrenaline and an equally high amount of risk. In recent years several motorcops from around the country have been killed in horrific accidents while escorting a presidential motorcade. It's some of the most hazardous duty a motorcop can endure. And we all love doing it.

Motorcops take great pride in their work and what better forum to demonstrate our skills and dedication than before a dignitary, and especially The President of the United States? It doesn't matter whether you voted for the guy or not, it's an honor to be there helping to protect and transport such an important person. And we do all the work, too. There are no Secret Service motorcops. It all falls to the local police to ensure these things go off without a hitch.

And it's not only presidents and other politicians we escort. I also escorted the Pope. Twice!

It was September of 1987 and Pope John Paul II was coming to Phoenix of all places. The Southwest is loaded with Catholics, and Phoenix has as many as any city. The Pope's visit was a big deal, and the media could speak of nothing else for weeks prior to the visit. And we started planning a month in advance.

His was going to be a whirlwind visit that would tax us all to the breaking point. He was to land early in the morning at Sky Harbor Airport and hit the ground running. He had several visits planned during the morning before ending up, around noon, at the Saint Mary's basilica in downtown Phoenix to make a public address. Not only would the actual route be difficult to prepare and secure but there was always the chance he would make a last-minute schedule change that would send us all scurrying.

Saint Mary's has a large balcony on the second floor of its south wall, which faced a huge courtyard next to Phoenix City Plaza. There was room for thousands of people to congregate there to hear the Pope's address and beginning days ahead of time, tens of thousands did just that. I'd never seen such a crowd. There were people as far as I could see. Happy people. Everyone seemed happy to be there and many were so happy they were in tears. It was actually kind of moving, even for a hard-boiled cop like me. Which brings me to the cool part of the story.

I was stationed at a fixed post for the end of this leg of the escort for the Pope. I think this leg consisted of escorting the Pope from a local hospital to Saint Mary's for the address. The first part of the day the Pope was in a simple limousine as he stopped to visit church officials and made his other morning stops. For the trip from the hospital to Saint Mary's he switched to his Popemobile so the crowd could see him. The majority of his morning itinerary was not widely publicized but the stop at the hospital, followed by the visit to Saint Mary's, was and the route between the two was jam packed with people. The Pope was a people person and apparently wanted to wave at folks along this section of the route, hence the use of the Popemobile. The Popemobile was a custom made Mercedes truck, which had a large, elevated glass box perched on top, which gave the Pope an elevated view and, more importantly, let the crowd see him as he drove by.

I had a traffic post near the beginning of this leg of the trip and when the motorcade passed, I had to hustle to the intersection of Third Street and Van Buren to attend my fixed post. Both Third Street and Van Buren Street were closed to traffic, but I was stationed here for crowd control along with several other motorcops. The Pope's motorcade would come east on Van Buren then turn right onto southbound Third Street before turning into the rear parking lot of Saint Mary's. As with every other square inch of ground anywhere near Saint Mary's there were thousands of people near this intersection. For the most part, they were very well behaved and reacted properly to all our instructions. When the Pope arrived, his Popemobile made its right turn without a hitch. To the delight of thousands of cheering fans the Pope waved energetically to all with his patented Pope wave, hands held outstretched with his palms turned slightly skyward.

That leads me to the cool part. The press had several fixed cameras set up along the route, as the local news channels broadcast most of the Pope's trip on live TV. We had several small areas roped off for press cameras and one of these roped-off areas was on the same corner of Third and Van Buren where I was standing. One of the press members in this area was a photographer for our local paper, the Arizona Republic who was standing next to and slightly behind me when he snapped the picture that would grace the front page of the next day's paper. And that's the cool part. On the front page of the next day's paper was a full page photo of the Pope standing in his Popemobile and looking directly at me, in the photo's foreground, holding out his hands as if to say hello. It was a neat shot and copies of it floated around the station for months. Most had handwritten captions such as 'Hey Tim, Long Time No See!' and the like. I was even asked to autograph a couple of them. I guess everyone gets his or her fifteen minutes, one way or another.

The Pope addressed the crowd for about an hour and made everyone in attendance very happy. Afterwards, the escort duties got pretty interesting and even more dangerous. At the time, the Pope's people were pretty concerned for his safety. It was only a few years prior that someone shot the guy four times right in front of Saint Peter's Square. They were, understandably, a bit security conscious. I'm not sure if they still do this today but in 1984 they ran two identical Popemobiles during certain parts of their motorcades. My second escort of the Pope was during this decoy phase.

In the late afternoon, the Pope was traveling from downtown Phoenix to Sun Devil Stadium on the Campus of Arizona State University in Tempe. This was the longest motorcade of his trip and would cover about 20 miles through heavy traffic. This part of the route was not publicized so there was little anticipation of much crowd control needed along the route. Still, Popemobiles attract attention wherever they go so the decision was made to run two separate motorcades along two separate routes using two different Popemobiles. They both left Saint Mary's about a minute apart. One took surface streets the entire distance and the other, the one I was on, took the freeway. Once we arrived at Sun Devil Stadium, we were relieved by Tempe motorcops so we never got to see which motorcade the Pope was actually in. I later heard the freeway motorcade had the actual Pope in it (he obviously rode in one of the darkened limos, and not atop his Popemobile during the trip).

In addition to the Pope, I escorted President Reagan, his wife Nancy, President Bush, his wife Barbara, Vice President Quayle, President Clinton, Vice President Gore and his wife, Tipper. The Reagans and the Quayles were frequent visitors because they had family in town. I always looked forward to President Reagan coming to town because he was a very friendly guy and always took the time to talk to us. I liked Vice President Quayle for the same reason. I'm not sure I was that fond of Quayle as a politician, but he was a very nice guy and had a personable way about him. Just like President Reagan, he seemed to be genuinely appreciative of the great service we gave him when he visited our town. And we gave them all the very best service we could. There was no group of motorcops in the world who gave better service to a dignitary than the motorcycle officers of the Phoenix Police Department.

Does that mean these dignitary details were all fun and exciting? Were dignitaries always fun to escort?

No.

One time it almost killed me. And got me on the front page again!

Sir Charles

It was 1993 and the NBA championship ended with a whimper for Phoenix Suns fans. When John Paxson's three-pointer found nothing but net to end game six and clinch the title for the Chicago Bulls we, as Suns fans, were devastated. And there were lots of Suns fans too. Like most Arizonans, I am a life-long fan of the Phoenix Suns, and the loss was a crush. The Suns hadn't been to the finals since 1976 when they suffered a heartbreaking loss to the Boston Celtics. Although we were going up against the storied Michael Jordan era Bulls, and no one gave us much of a chance, we faithful fans still had hope, right up to the end.

Even though we lost, there was such Suns fever surrounding the 1993 season that there had to be something we could do to show our appreciation for a great season and a hard-fought final series.

Paul Johnson was affectionately known as the 'Boy Mayor' of Phoenix, because he was the youngest mayor in the city's history and because, at 30 years old, looked like he was a teenager. Mayor Johnson decided to have a Suns Appreciation Parade in downtown Phoenix to celebrate the season. It was a hurriedly planned event scheduled in the first days following the Sun's loss. The parade would start at the State capitol and run down Jefferson Street to the then-new America West Arena at 5th Street and Jefferson. It was a relatively short and straight route, and no one expected any problems. When the parade reached the arena the players would go inside and address the crowd from the beautiful elevated balcony of the Copper Club restaurant. After a few remarks to the crowd, the event would be over.

We scheduled what we thought would be plenty of officers to line the route and work the crowd. In addition to the hundred or so motorcops, there would be downtown walking beat officers, SWAT officers, public relations officers and a smattering of regular beat cops. In all we were probably 250 strong and expected about 30,000-50,000 people to attend.

It was June 26th and was the hottest day of 1993 so far. The parade was scheduled to start around 9:00AM and when the first of us arrived around 6:00AM to prepare the route, there were already nearly 100,000 people lining the 2.5 mile route.

We were in trouble and we knew it.

As the parade time grew closer, the crowd grew larger. The call went out to the State Police and the Capitol Police for reinforcements but there was nothing we could do but hope for the best. By the time the parade started there were 300,000 people lining the short parade route. We were simply overwhelmed by 10 times more crowd then we planned for. There was little we could do to keep the crowd out of the street. From the very beginning, it was bedlam.

My post was directly in front of the arena. The plan was for the players, riding in their classic, open cars to wave at the crowd until they arrived at the arena. Once out front they would stroll into the arena, which was closed to the public, and ride the elevator up to the Copper Club. Once inside the club they'd come onto the balcony to address the crowd.

The parade started late. The cars the players were to ride in were having trouble getting through to the staging area. The crowds at that end were huge and the cries over the police radio indicated we were in for a bad time. They were doing their best on that end but things were rough. It wasn't much better on our end either. Most of the crowd was congregated around the arena, and we were having a tough time keeping the road clear. We wanted to keep the people on the sidewalks but there were simply not enough sidewalks to hold everyone. They were spilling into the street, and we were forced to deal with them.

They hadn't overwhelmed us quite yet and although they were spilling into the roadway, Jefferson Street is nearly 80 feet wide in front of the arena, and it looked like there would still be enough room to safely get the players and their cars through the crowd.

Don Sanderson owned the oldest Ford dealership in Arizona and had an outstanding personal collection of vintage Fords. He brought several of them to the parade for players to ride in. They were all convertibles and the players were to sit atop the back seats and wave at the crowd as they passed. The finest car in Don's collection that day was an original Shelby Cobra. A stunning and well preserved car, the Cobra was priceless and was reserved for the star of the Phoenix Suns, Charles Barkley. It would be the lead car in the parade and the first to arrive at my location at the end of the parade route in front of the arena. It was the last day this particular Cobra would be an unmolested original show car.

When the parade got started things went quickly downhill. The plan was to have the cars travel at only 1-2 miles per hour, going slowly along the route, to give the fans ample time to cheer. Shortly after the parade began, we heard the radio shouts from the officers to have the cars speed up. The cars were going too slowly, and the crowd was rushing them as they passed. It was hoped that, at a speed of about 5-10 miles per hour, the cars would be less attractive to the surging crowd. And it worked, for a few minutes.

Once the lead car, with Charles Barkley aboard, arrived in front of the arena the crowd overwhelmed us and flowed unstoppably into the street. There were about six of us on motorcycles stationed at the end of the route. We were standing next to our bikes as we waited for the cars to arrive, but it looked like we might have to make a hasty exit. When we saw the crowd's reaction to the approaching cars, we decided to keep the cars moving past the front of the arena, away from the crowd. We would hurry them down to 7th Street, away from the largest part of the crowd, and into the arena the back way.

At least that was the plan.

As the cars got close several of us got onto our bikes and formed a box in the middle of Jefferson Street for the lead car to drive into. Once the car was flanked by four motorcops we would continue east, without stopping, until we got to 7th Street.

And it almost worked.

The only problem was we had no way to warn the driver of the Cobra about the change in plans. We tried our best to relay our plan to the rest of the officers nearest us but the crowd was so noisy and things were so hectic, no one got word to the driver. We decided to use hand gestures and shout at the tops of our lungs when he got close, but it was no use. When the Cobra reached us, with a very frightened looking driver and an even more frightened looking Charles Barkley, the driver could see that he was to drive into the opened area we were maintaining in the middle of the road. By the time he reached us the crowd was on the move and our attempts to signal him to keep moving weren't understood. The driver of the Cobra pulled up between us, with two motorcops astride idling motorcycles on each side and as he'd been instructed to do at the beginning of the parade, stopped the car.

The crowd was on us in an instant. The press of the crowd was enormous, and before I knew it I was pinned hard against the driver's side of the Cobra. The motorcop behind me and the two on the passenger side of the Cobra were, likewise, pinned against the car. There we were, sitting astride our running bikes, leaning into the unprotected sides of a priceless antique roadster, being pressed by the weight of thousands of straining people.

I've been a cop for a long, long time. I've been shot at, stabbed, beaten, kicked and run over by a parade float but this was the closest I'd ever come to being killed in the line of duty.

I was immobilized. My right leg was pinned between the car and my bike and my left leg was pinned hard against the bike by the crowd. I could hear people scream in pain as they pressed bare skin against the red-hot metal of my motorcycle's engine and searing hot exhaust system, but still they pressed against us. After a few seconds, I could feel the metal of the car give way under the intense pressure of my leg and motorcycle being pressed deeper and deeper into the side of the car. My right hip was forced against the windshield frame of the Cobra and as the pressure grew the windshield shattered from the growing pressure of the crowd. I managed to keep my hands free and as did my brothers on their bikes, tried to push back at the crowd. We hollered against impossible noise trying to get people to move away from the car. Finally, a hastily gathered group of about 15 officers forced their way through the crowd and up to the Cobra.

I strained to turn my smashed body around to see what was happening. The crowd was clawing at poor Charles Barkley, as if they wanted a souvenir of flesh from the guy. And he was petrified. I don't think I've ever seen a man so scared and certain of an impending, awful death as I did that day. He was about to be killed by this mob, and he knew it. Fortunately, before the crowd could kill him, the officers reached him and pulled him from the car. Literally beating their way through the crowd, these officers dragged Charles from the car and across the 200 feet of suddenly ugly landscape to the safety of the arena.

Then, almost as quickly as it attacked us, the crowd retreated, and we were saved. Their star player was gone, and they had little interest in the Cobra, or being in the street with us. The rest of the players were saved too. Some of the cars managed to turn off Jefferson and go around before being mobbed. The others were pulled from the cars and escorted to safety.

The best part? Everyone lived. There were plenty of injured people and police officers, but nothing too serious.

The next morning there was a cool picture in the paper, and my second time on the front page. There was a photographer on the Copper Club balcony that had an elevated, front row seat of the Malay. From his vantagepoint he snapped a great picture of the crowd crushing the Cobra, with a near-death Charles Barkley inside and a mad-as-hell looking Motor officer pinned against the car.

Devon

I knew Fred for many years. We were friends and rode Motors together. As it happens with long-term friendships, you tend to lose some track of time. I remember being surprised when Fred told me his son, Devon, had a new driver's license and was looking for some transportation. It didn't seem possible at the time. After all, Devon was just a little boy the last time I saw him.

Sure enough, Devon was a driver now and needed some wheels. Since I always seemed to have a project or two at the house, friends regularly came to me in hopes of finding a decent deal on a used car. The only problem I had with Fred's request was I didn't have a car for sale at the time. What I did have was a motorcycle.

Guy was another friend who bought a Suzuki GS850 brand new, sometime in the 1980s. He rode it sparingly and, after a few years, kinda got tired of it. As so many seem to do, he parked it alongside the house under a tarp and forgot about it. One day, while at Guy's house, I spotted it and asked about it. Guy said it had low miles on it and ran fine when he parked it, but it hadn't been started in years. One thing led to another and Guy agreed to part with the Suzuki. The next thing I knew I had a weathered old bike on my carport.

I was no stranger to fixing old, weathered bikes. In Arizona a bike gets old and weathered in no time, especially if left outdoors. I've seen bikes almost destroyed beyond repair after only one summer left outside. The heat simply destroys any plastic or rubber pieces, reduces fabric to tatters and burns away paint. Fortunately, Guy's bike was stored on the shady side of his 2-story house and under a stout, canvas tarp. That doesn't mean it was well preserved. All the rubber and plastic parts were shot but the seat and paint were still in good shape.

Once I had the bike home, I started the painstaking process of disassembling every part that contained a rubber gasket or seal. They all had to be inspected and replaced, if necessary, so brakes, carburetors, clutches and the like all came apart and were refurbished. The wiring was all disconnected, cleaned and reassembled. Relays were cleaned and tested, dry-rotted tires and fork gaiters were replaced, and new foot peg and grip rubbers were installed. It was a time consuming project, but I love doing that kind of thing and was always happy to have a project like this to occupy my free time.

Cop work is tough and I needed this type of hobby.

I worked on the bike for a few weeks and was just at the point it was road worthy. I took it for several test rides and was dealing with the inevitable fine-tuning necessary after such a project. The bike was mechanically in pretty sound shape, and my next step was to address the cosmetic issues. There were many chrome pieces that needed cleaning and polishing. The seat needed a deep cleaning and dressing. The paint also needed a good polish to bring back its factory shine. It wouldn't be long before the GS850 was finished.

This was what I told Fred. I didn't have a car I could sell Devon, but I told Fred I had Guy's old motorcycle nearly ready for sale. I know what you're thinking. I'm a father too. Who wants their kid's first car to be a motorcycle? What kind of monster am I, anyway? How could I possibly suggest to Fred that he consider letting his precious young son have a motorcycle?

Get over it.

Men are men, and Motors are Motors. Fred was a Motor and Devon was a young man. If I have to explain much more than that, you will never understand. Maybe it's a guy thing, or maybe it's a macho thing. Motorcycles appeal to men and motorcycles definitely appeal to young, newly licensed men. I know Devon wanted a car, and I didn't blame him. As cool as a bike would be it really isn't practical for everyday transportation. Even with an average of over 300 sunny days a year in Arizona there are still times when motorcycling is out of the question. However, especially for a first timer, the idea sounds terrific.

Remember that my first car was a motorcycle. I rode it rain or shine. I even devised ways to carry things around on it. My friend Russell even used his to go to the golf course by slinging his bag full of clubs over his shoulder.

Anyway, all I had to offer Fred was the Suzuki, and he seemed really interested. He hadn't considered a motorcycle until I mentioned it, and now he thought it might be a good idea. He'd tell Devon and let me know. A few days later I was making arrangements to meet Devon at the house and show him the Suzuki.

In the meantime, I finished the detailing on the bike, and it turned out great. It was nice and shiny and ran perfectly. Don't get me wrong. A GS850 is not a particularly attractive motorcycle. It's not a sport bike like the ever-popular Ninja. It wasn't a tour bike either. It was what was commonly referred to at the time as a Japanese Standard. It was a plain looking bike and had rather bulky looking lines to it. Although there was nothing particularly wrong with the way it looked, it definitely wasn't going to win any beauty contests. When I finally stepped back to look at it after it was finished, I thought it looked kinda frumpy. I couldn't imagine Devon would like it very much, especially when most kids his age that rode motorcycles had knee-dragging, fire-breathing sport bikes.

That's not to say the Suzuki was not a fast bike. What it lacked in good looks it made up for in power. I had an excellent engine that made gobs of power. It also handled quite well for a Standard. I had a feeling if Devon could see past the looks of the bike and took a ride on it he'd be sold. As it turned out, I needn't have been concerned.

Fred and Devon came over to the house one afternoon, and the bike was sitting outside waiting for them, gleaming in the mid-day Arizona sunshine. For a frumpy bike, it still looked good in its newly polished paint and chrome. And Devon loved it. I think, especially with Dad footing the bill, Devon would have liked anything short of a pink, 50cc scooter. And I knew how he felt. I remembered what it was like to be so anxious to have my own set of wheels, and I also remember how excited I was the first time I rode a motorcycle. I envied Devon the fun and adventure waiting for him.

As with me, some 25 years before, Devon didn't have any real motorcycle riding experience. That didn't stop him from ogling the bike from all angles and sitting on it while daydreaming of flying down the road, free as a bird. I knew the minute he stepped from the car and looked at the Suzuki that he would be its next owner.

Devon didn't ride so Dad did the test ride. We were used to riding fast bikes so the Suzuki had a lot to live up to with Fred riding it. And it performed very well. Fred came back from his ride and pronounced the bike fit for his son. It wasn't long before I was waving to Fred, riding down the street on the Suzuki, followed in their car by Devon.

I must admit I felt a tiny bit of apprehension about selling a large, powerful motorcycle to a new rider. I can imagine Bill felt the same way 25 years ago when he sold me the Honda. I just hoped, as I watched them pull away, that Devon would enjoy the Suzuki as much as I enjoyed that Honda. Who knows, one day he might be writing cool stories about his motorcycles and lead off with one about the guy who sold him his first bike.

Vern

Vern and I are good friends who met on the Police Department shortly after Vern graduated from the academy. We always knew who each other were but never actually worked much together until Vern transferred to Motors. I'd been a Motor for years and as was customary, we all took Vern under our wings a bit and helped him learn the ropes.

Vern was good at being a Motor and took to it quickly. Aside from being a good cop, and an affable guy, he could also ride. This made his affliction all the more puzzling.

Vern had the worst luck of any Motor I ever knew. I don't think I knew anyone so unlucky astride a bike. Vern crashed his Police motorcycle more times than any motor I ever knew. And it all seemed to be a matter of sheer, dumb luck.

If a freak burst of wind caught a Motor during a dust storm, and knocked him over, it would be Vern. If a drunk were going to pull out, directly in the path of an oncoming Motor, that Motor would be Vern. If a sudden water main break flooded a blind corner, the next Motor to round the bend, and go down, would be Vern. It was amazing and seemed to worry everyone but Vern himself.

Vern is a big man and can take a beating better than almost anyone. Even though he crashed with great regularity, he never seemed to get hurt too badly. Some stitches, maybe a broken bone or some road rashes were not enough to discourage Vern. He loved to ride and was a fast healer. Despite the gremlins that followed him on every shift, he always came back for more. This wasn't uncommon. It took a lot more than a wreck to discourage most Motors from returning to the job. We all had our crashes, and we all bounced back from them. Damn it though, it sure seemed Vern had way more than his share.

In all of Vern's crashes I can only remember him getting seriously hurt one time. And I was right there with him when it happened.

We were working a drag racing complaint in the Ahwatukee Foothills area of South Phoenix. This is the extreme south part of town and is bordered by Indian Reservation and open desert. The farthest south paved roadway in Phoenix is Pecos Road, which runs East and West along the southern border of Ahwatukee.

Ahwatukee is a rather upscale part of town and consists of mostly newer homes. Owners of these upscale homes value the remoteness of Ahwatukee and seem to favor the peace and quiet that normally accompanies this remoteness.

Kids like remoteness too, especially when it comes at the end of a 6-mile stretch of 4-lane blacktop at the very edge of town. Kids like the extreme western dead end of Pecos Road for late night keggers and bonfires. It's about a half-mile to the nearest home and, as long as they're not too noisy, they generally don't generate many complaints. When the kids added drag racing to their activities, that all changed.

Nothing's noisier than a bunch of kids drag racing. Drinking, shouting, playing loud music and racing loud cars all combine for a Police headache. We handled repeated complaints on Pecos Road of the noise, but it was a hard area to respond to. Pecos Road was several miles long, straight as a string, and ended in a dead end. The kids could see us coming for miles and would disperse, either in the oncoming direction, up to one of the nearby side streets or off into the desert. We were always able to run them off, but we were seldom able to catch any of them.

One bright full-moon lit night Vern and I were working the Ahwatukee area when a call came out of a loud noise disturbing in the area of 7th Avenue and Pecos Road. Vern and I were close and advised Radio we would take the call. We pulled off the road and decided to develop some sort of strategy before going down Pecos Road. As we brainstormed we could hear the roar of loud car exhausts even though were we a good 2 miles away. We finally came up with a plan.

Vern and I decided to get as close to the end of Pecos Road as we could, using side streets. This still left several miles of the dark, unlit open road we'd have to cross to get anywhere near them. Since there was a full moon we decided to turn off all our lights and drive slowly towards the dead end, hopefully without being seen. We'd then park in the median, radar guns at the ready and hopefully catch a couple drag racers before the whole group spotted us and scattered.

We did just that. Serenaded by the unmistakable sounds of racing cars and shouting kids, we drove, lights out, west down Pecos Road until we were close enough to see a group of about a dozen kids and as many cars. There were also a couple of motorcycles in the bunch. We parked in the median and waited.

We didn't have to wait long. After just a few minutes sitting in the dark the kids at the end of the road got ready for the next race. Two motorcycles pulled up to the line on the eastbound side of the median, facing our direction. Just like in a bad 1960s teen rebel movie, a girl in a skirt stepped out ahead of the two wildly revving motorcycles. She raised a light colored piece of cloth above her head for a few seconds and then, suddenly, with a downward thrust, sent the motorcycles hurdling toward us.

We were ready for them. Radar guns poised. We read off the speeds silently to ourselves; 95, 100, 105, 110 and climbing. We had to be quick. There wasn't time to let them get to full speed before we put our guns in our saddlebags and prepared for the chase. We knew when they passed us these bikes would be well in excess of 125 miles per hour. If we had any hope of catching them from a standing start, we needed an edge.

Part of our plan included a scheme to slow them down. We decided we would wait until they were about 100 yards from us then we would light up every strobe and light bulb our bikes had. That, and a long, loud burst from our sirens, would certainly shock the shit out of these racers. As we figured it, they'd hit the brakes hard and be easier to catch. Besides, it would be cool to see the looks on their faces when they realized they'd been caught!

It worked perfectly. We were about a mile from the starting line, and these bikes were traveling as fast as they were able. When they were about a hundred yards out we fired up our bikes and lit the lights, adding a bunch of screeching siren. Both riders saw us at the same time and smashed on their brakes, sitting up slightly in their seats to brace against being thrust forward by the force of the slowing bikes. There was no way for them to stop from their high speed before they reached us, but they did slow significantly as they passed us. Pulling out from the median and chasing them down was going to be a cinch.

I was on Vern's left as we sat in the median, so I made the left turn onto the road first. I took off after the bike on the right, and Vern took off after the bike on the left. As I gained on my bike, he was already slowing down and looking back at me over his left shoulder. This wasn't going too much of a chase as my guy slowed to a stop along the right shoulder. Vern's guy, however, was going to make a fight of it.

As I pulled to a stop, Vern's racer decided to make a run for it. He recovered quickly from the initial shock of seeing us and, even though he'd slowed to about 40 miles per hour, he didn't pull over. Instead, he hit the gas and started to run with Vern hot on his tail. Just as I walked up to my stopped racer, Vern was flying by me after his racer.

I paused for a moment while my racer dug for his license. I watched as Vern rapidly gained on the other bike. Just as Vern pulled within about 100 feet of the other bike, the second racer did something completely unexpected. He pulled toward the center of the road then hit the brakes as hard as he could. As Vern did the same, the second racer made a hard, left turn, heading for the median. He was going to try and make it across in an attempt to get away.

The racer was riding a much more maneuverable bike than Vern. Loaded with enough gear to make them tip the scales at nearly 700 pounds, Kawasaki Police bikes were better at going straight than at stopping and turning. No matter how skilled Vern was, his bike was incapable of slowing and swerving adequately at that speed to avoid the race bike. Before the racer could make it to the median, and while he was perpendicular across the high beam of Vern's bike, they collided.

Vern smashed headlong into the left side of the racer. With a huge cloud of dirt, smoke and exploding fiberglass, parts and riders flew through the air. They seemed to be combined as one together, as if collected into a mass like so much dust from a passing whirlwind. The whole mass flew along before finally landing in the left lane and sliding along the road. As they slid, the two bikes and riders separated. Vern and his bike came to rest in the median. The other bike and rider came to rest still on the blacktop.

I grabbed my racer's license, which he held in his outstretched hand. Cramming it into my pocket I was astride my bike and alongside

Vern in seconds. I stopped my bike on the pavement near the downed racer. I could see he was out, lying face down on the pavement. After screaming into the radio for help, I ran past the fallen racer and into the median to check on my friend.

Vern was lying on his back looking straight up at the sky. He was conscious and although obviously hurt, I knew he was going to make it.

"Vern! You okay? Where are you hurt?"

"All over, but I'm still alive."

"Lay still, man. Help's on the way"

At about that time we could hear the beautiful sound of far off sirens. Despite our remote location, the call for help got out and everyone close enough to respond was on their way. I could also hear the not-so-beautiful sound of approaching engines. The kids from the end of the street, close enough to see something was wrong at our end, were on the way. I went to the other rider to check on him before the kids reached us. I didn't know what to expect when they got there, but I knew, for a few minutes at least, I was all alone to deal with them.

I reached the other biker and could see him still lying face down, moving slightly and making groaning noises. His helmet was smashed and rotated about halfway around his head, obstructing his face. I could tell he was breathing and decided to let him lie still. I noticed the racer I pulled over was now standing nearby.

"We need to get his helmet off," he shouted.

"Leave him alone. Help's coming."

"No! I'm getting his helmet. He can't breathe!"

The kid made a lunge for his downed friend, and I grabbed his arm to stop him. I explained to him it was important the helmet remained in place until the paramedics arrived. I assured him I already checked, and he was breathing on his own. With a nod to indicate he understood, he watched me walk to the center of the street to confront the approaching cars full of kids.

The first few cars that reached us simply slowed down and looked out the windows at us as they drove slowly past and disappeared down the road. The few that did stop discharged their passengers but, for the most part, they seemed pretty calm. Maybe they were in a bit of shock, but they simply gathered in a wide circle and stood looking at the mess of broken motorcycles and broken riders.

Suddenly, we were bathed in light. There was a helicopter approaching and had its huge, powerful spot lights trained directly on us. I hadn't realized how dark it was out there until the helicopter lit us up. Before he got there the only light was my flashlight, my motorcycle's headlight and the full moon.

I felt good enough about the crowd to stay in the median with Vern until the first units arrived. I put my racer in command of ensuring nobody tried to move the other rider until help arrived.

"Did I kill him?" Vern asked.

"No, he's still alive."

"Thank God. I thought I killed him."

"He's worse off than you" I said, "but I think he's gonna make it."

I knew how he felt. I remembered the time about ten years earlier when I hit a kid and thought I killed him.

The first emergency unit to arrive was an ambulance operated by Fire Department Paramedics. Before long we had several cops and paramedics around to help us. We got statements from some of the kids that stayed behind and got to work reconstructing the scene for the inevitable paperwork that would follow. I was particularly interested in getting the downed racer's driver's license before he was transported to the hospital. They have a way of disappearing, and I wanted it firmly in my pocket. I knew it could be some time before I got to the hospital.

I walked over to the ambulance as they were loading the downed racer inside. I asked the Medic if he got any ID from him yet. With that he handed me the driver's license he took from the kid's wallet. It was brand new and its photo looked familiar.

It was Devon.

I asked the paramedic to hold on a minute. I climbed into the ambulance and got my first look at the racer. It was Devon all right. His helmet was off now, and I could clearly see his face. He was awake, breathing on his own, but still not talking. I told him it would be okay, and I would call his Dad. With that he was secured in the ambulance and was off to the hospital.

The next few hours would be tough on everyone. My racer got a ticket for drag racing before I finally let him go. Vern was on his way to the hospital with injuries it would take him months to recover from. My other good friend's son was going to the hospital with even more serious injuries than Vern's. I would be consumed for hours writing this one up but the two worst things still had to be done. I had to call Fred and tell him what happened, and I had to go to the hospital and determine if Devon would survive long enough to write him a drag racing ticket.

Many weeks went by. Vern came back to work at light duty at the station while the injuries healed. Fred forgave me for selling his son the motorcycle that nearly killed him. Even Devon would come to forgive me for charging him with drag racing.

On the day of Devon's trial, he pleaded guilty. I was so happy to see him up and around and healing well from the accident. Vern and I both spoke to the Judge during his sentencing and told her what a fine man we knew Devon to be. I don't know how much it helped, but he did seem to get a slightly smaller than normal fine and, most importantly, no jail time.

Devon drove a car after that but also bought another motorcycle after giving Fred about a year to get over what happened. I run into Fred occasionally and always ask about Devon. Fred's as proud of his son as can be, and we're both glad he's still with us.

Conclusion

I've enjoyed recounting these old motorcycle stories, and I hope you enjoyed reading them. They were every bit as easy to write and maybe even just a bit more so than the ones in my first book, 'For Love of the Car'. Perhaps it's because I had a bit of writing experience under my belt, or maybe it was because I like these stories a tiny bit more.

It's a bit like being asked which of your children you like the best. Every parent gives the proper response that they love each of their children equally. We all claim to have no favorite when it comes to our kids. In truth, we probably don't love one kid more than another. We love them just a bit differently. I feel that way about the hundreds of cars and motorcycles I've owned over the years.

All together I think there are some things I love about motorcycles that I simply don't love as much about cars. I really enjoy going fast but the sensation is infinitely more enjoyable on a motorcycle. You just can't experience the sensation of speed in a car like you can astride a bike. I like working on motorcycles more than working on cars. It's just so much simpler and the rewards come more quickly.

Yeah, if I had to pick a favorite between cars and motorcycles I think I'd have to say out loud that I love them both the same. Silently, to myself, by the very slimmest of margins, I'm not sure that would be the answer.

Anyway, I fulfilled my promise to write down some of my motorcycle stories. So, what's next? Did I ever tell you I spent years as a bicycle mechanic and, for many years, built custom bicycles? Well, you never know. Maybe someday I will.

Lightning Source UK Ltd.
Milton Keynes UK
UKHW041159240621
386085UK00001B/22